THE
ARMY IN THE PACIFIC
A CENTURY OF ENGAGEMENT

by

James C. McNaughton

Center of Military History
United States Army
Washington, D.C., 2012

Published by Books Express Publishing
Copyright © Books Express, 2013
ISBN 978-1-78266-276-1

Books Express publications are available from all good retail and online booksellers. For
publishing proposals and direct ordering please contact us at: info@books-express.com

CONTENTS

ILLUSTRATIONS

Illustrations courtesy of the following sources: pp. 9, 10, Library of Congress; 15, U.S. Army Museum of Hawaii; 18, 53, National Archives; 28, 30, 38, U.S. Army Signal Corps; 45, 55, 68, U.S. Army Art Collection; 52, U.S. Navy; 67, U.S. Army; 70, U.S. Army Center of Military History; 79, 85, Department of Defense.

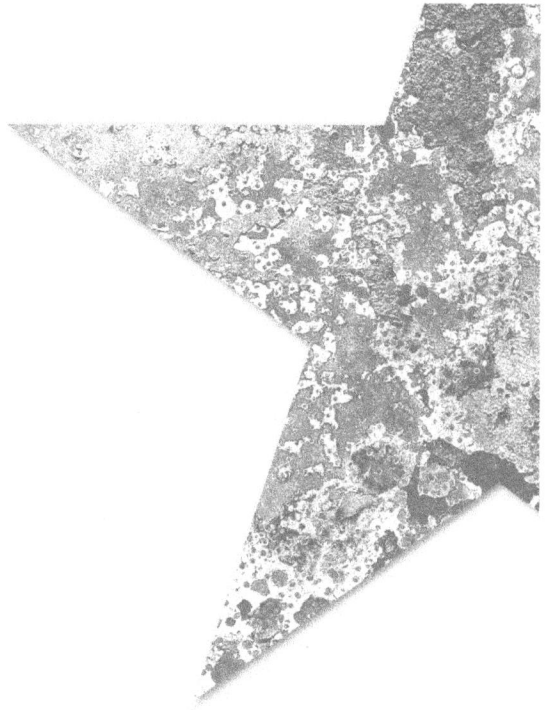

FOREWORD

The experiences of the U.S. Army in the Pacific provide significant insight into the complexity and uncertainty we face today. At a time when our Nation's leaders have called for a renewed emphasis on the Pacific, and many of our Soldiers have spent much of the last decade engaged in other parts of the world, it is important to review our long-standing engagement in this critical region. The Pacific has always played a significant role for the United States. Today, seven of ten of the largest armies in the world are in the Pacific and there are approximately 66,000 U.S. Soldiers stationed in the region. They are the modern day standard-bearers of an Army tradition dating back to 1803, when Lewis and Clark first gazed on the Pacific after leading the Corps of Discovery across the North American continent. In the future, this role will increase in significance as the Pacific becomes host to some of the world's largest populations, militaries, and economies. Whether it was the intense combat in World War II or disaster relief in northern Japan in 2011, the Army's experience in the Pacific is replete with lessons for the future.

As this work clearly illustrates, the Army has conducted almost every conceivable mission in the Pacific region. From training Philippine forces in the 1920s to working as part of an international force in the 1930s, the Army learned and adapted to changes in the environment. Changes in national requirements caused the Army to transition from intense combat in Korea and Vietnam in the 1950s and 1960s to training and building partner capacity in Thailand and Japan in the 1990s. Simply put, the Pacific experience illustrates the breadth of missions the U.S. Army has conducted and provides a useful backdrop for those the Army must be prepared for in the future.

The first chapter of this history describes the Army's forty-year engagement with the many diverse cultures, people, and languages of the Pacific. From these formative experiences rose Army leaders like Generals Marshall and MacArthur, who understood the complexity and interdependence of regions, cultures, and religions. In the future, as technology lowers barriers to communications and travel, building on a similarly well-developed understanding of the many dynamic factors present in this environment will be increasingly important.

The Pacific also provides examples of joint, interagency, inter-governmental, and multinational operations. From the first time U.S. Army Soldiers sailed to the Philippines on Navy ships, through joint amphibious operations in the central Pacific, to multinational opera-tions in the Korean Conflict and more recently, humanitarian relief operations in Japan, the Army has demonstrated the capability to operate in a joint, interagency, intergovernmental, and multinational environment. Soldiers and leaders can expect to build on these capa-bilities to provide the desired effects to achieve our Nation's objectives.

Most importantly, this history is a timely reminder that change is the nature of the Army profession. The second and third chapters, dealing with World War II and the Cold War, relate the complex chal-lenges the Army faced as former adversaries became partners and transnational terrorists threatened the world order. The Army's experi-ence in the Pacific serves as a reminder that the only thing certain is the unexpected.

Soldiers should read this history with pride and honor in the long tradition of service that they now carry forward. I expect that leaders will use this volume to develop challenging professional development vignettes to generate perspective and context for our combat-proven Soldiers. Our Pacific history is one of both valor and strength, and provides the inspiration to secure our Nation's future.

Washington, D.C.
16 August 2012

RAYMOND T. ODIERNO
General, United States Army

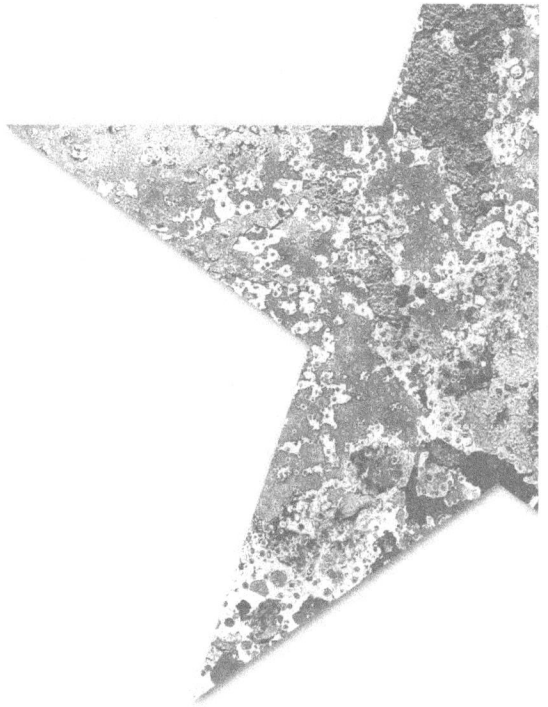

THE AUTHOR

James C. McNaughton is chief of the Contemporary Studies Branch, Histories Division, U.S. Army Center of Military History. He previously served as the command historian for several Army and Joint commands, including the U.S. Army, Pacific. He received a B.A. degree from Middlebury College, Vermont, and M.A. and Ph.D. degrees in history from Johns Hopkins University, Baltimore, Maryland. He has served as an officer in the Active Army, National Guard, and Army Reserve, and as an Army civilian. He is the author of *Nisei Linguists: Japanese Americans in the Military Intelligence Service during World War II* (2006).

INTRODUCTION

For the first century or more of its existence, the U.S. Army served the nation as a continental army for an expanding country. But in 1898, America unexpectedly expanded overseas and its Army changed into a global expeditionary force. The War with Spain pushed America first into the Caribbean but then with more enduring results into the Asia-Pacific region. Most Americans called this region the Far East, even though in some ways it could be considered the westward extension of the American frontier. As on the frontier, in this complex region the Army would be called upon for a variety of missions, from counterinsurgency and nation building to major combat and deterrence. Over the next century, the Army would experience there some of its greatest successes and greatest disappointments.

Several experiences foreshadowed the Army's future in the region. American seafaring merchants had first become involved in the China trade as early as 1784. But it was the Louisiana Purchase that drew the Army toward the Pacific. In 1804, President Thomas Jefferson sent two experienced infantry officers, Capt. Meriwether Lewis and 2d Lt. William Clark, to explore the new territory and reconnoiter a path across the continent. Their expedition, also known as the Corps of Discovery, traveled up the

Missouri River from St. Louis with thirty-four soldiers and twelve contract boatmen. Eighteen months and more than four thousand miles later, they reached the mouth of the Columbia River. "Great joy in camp," Clark wrote in his journal, "we are in *View* of the *Ocian*, this great Pacific Octean which we been So long anxious to See [spelling and emphasis in the original]." But the excitement did not last. They built winter quarters and waited out the dreary rain and unfriendly natives of the Pacific Northwest. The following year, they returned home to a hero's welcome. The expedition established America's first foothold on the shores of the Pacific and demonstrated to the young nation that it had what came to be called a "manifest destiny," a mission to spread its civilization across the continent. Henceforth, America would face not just the Atlantic Ocean but the Pacific as well. To protect America's growing commerce and whaling in the region, the U.S. Navy established the Pacific Squadron in 1821.

The Army's next Pacific encounter came in 1846 when war broke out between the United States and Mexico, and the Pacific Squadron seized ports in Alta California. To hold the new territory, President James K. Polk sent soldiers by land and sea. Col. Stephen W. Kearny led a mounted force from Fort Leavenworth, Kansas, to Santa Fe and then onward over the Rocky Mountains. There, Kearny's three hundred regulars linked up with a detachment of sailors and marines to fight the Californios at San Pascual and take San Diego and Los Angeles. Meanwhile, the War Department sent Company F, 3d Artillery, by sea around Cape Horn into the Pacific. "Swords were brought out, guns oiled and made ready, and every thing was in a bustle, when the old *Lexington* dropped her anchor on January 26, 1847, in Monterey Bay," wrote 1st Lt. William T. Sherman, "after a voyage of 198 days from New York." By that time, the fighting had already ended and its mission changed to establishing a military government over the large province. In 1848, gold was discovered near Sacramento, and the soldiers maintained order until California won statehood in 1850. By the time the transcontinental railroad was completed in 1869, America had expanded "from sea to shining sea."

For the rest of the century, the United States saw itself drawn further into the Pacific, with the Navy as its principal instrument. The Army had only a secondary role. In 1853, the Navy sent Commodore Matthew C. Perry to open Japan to American trade. In 1867, when the United States purchased Alaska from Russia, the

War Department sent Battery H, 2d Artillery, and Company F, 9th Infantry, to Sitka to take possession. In 1871, when Korean coastal forts fired on U.S. Navy ships, the Asiatic Squadron conducted punitive raids with sailors and marines. In 1872, the secretary of war sent the commander of the Military Division of the Pacific, Maj. Gen. John M. Schofield, and his chief engineer, Lt. Col. Barton S. Alexander, to the Kingdom of Hawaii for "ascertaining the defensive capabilities of the various ports and their commercial facilities." The two officers recommended that the United States acquire a quiet lagoon named Pearl Harbor. Hawaii granted rights to Pearl Harbor in 1887, but Congress did not appropriate funds for dredging until after Hawaii became a U.S. territory. In 1878, the United States signed a treaty for a South Pacific coaling station with the Kingdom of Samoa. In 1893, the Pacific Squadron put ashore in Hawaii a landing party of one hundred sixty sailors and marines to protect a junta of Americans who had overthrown the Hawaiian monarchy. In 1897, the War Department sent troops to provide security for the Klondike gold fields in Alaska. By the 1890s, the United States had expanding interests in the Asia-Pacific region, but was not yet a Pacific power. No one yet envisioned a major role for the Army in this maritime theater.

AN ARMY FOR EMPIRE, 1898–1941

THE WAR WITH SPAIN AND THE PHILIPPINE WAR, 1898–1902

In early 1898, Spain's harsh counterinsurgency campaign on Cuba caused tensions with the United States. In January, as a show of force, the Navy deployed the USS *Maine* to Havana. On 15 February, while riding at anchor in the harbor, the battleship exploded with a loss of two hundred sixty men. Americans instantly blamed Spain. Although proof was lacking, on 25 April Congress declared war. For the first time since the Civil War, the War Department went on a war footing and tens of thousands of volunteers flocked to the colors. At the same time on the other side of the world, the U.S. Navy's Asiatic Squadron sailed from Hong Kong to destroy the Spanish squadron in Manila Bay. Commodore George Dewey accomplished this easily, then telegraphed Washington to send soldiers. Naval power, he said, could "reach no further ashore. For tenure of the land you must have the man with a rifle."

President William McKinley chose a veteran of the Civil War and Indian Wars, Maj. Gen. Wesley Merritt, to organize and lead the U.S. Army's VIII Corps to the Philippines "for the twofold purpose of completing the reduction of Spanish power . . . and of giving order and security to the islands while in the possession of the

0   150

Miles

SOUTH CHINA SEA

BABUYAN IS.

LUZON

Fort Stotsenburg

BATAAN

Subic Bay

Manila

Corregidor

Fort William McKinley

Manila Bay

0   25

Miles

PHILIPPINE SEA

Manila

MINDORO

MASBATE

SAMAR

VISAYAN ISLANDS

PANAY

LEYTE

Balangiga

CEBU

PALAWAN

BOHOL

NEGROS

SULU SEA

MINDANAO

BASILAN

SULU

Sulu Archipelago

NORTH BORNEO

CELEBES SEA

Map 1

United States." At the Presidio of San Francisco, Merritt assembled and trained two thousand regulars and thirteen thousand volunteers. The first contingent sailed from San Francisco on 25 May, stopping at Honolulu and Guam along the way. When Congress voted in July to annex Hawaii, the War Department sent the 1st New York Volunteers and the 3d Battalion, 2d U.S. Volunteer Engineers, to garrison the strategically located islands.

When the first soldiers arrived in Manila on 30 June, after more than a month at sea, they found a revolutionary army of some thirteen thousand Filipinos led by Emilio Aguinaldo besieging the Spanish troops inside Intramuros, the walled city in Manila. The rebels had struggled against Spanish rule for years and hoped the Americans had come to help them gain independence. Instead, American commanders conducted talks directly with the Spanish commander. After six weeks of waiting, the VIII Corps attacked Manila on 13 August in a heavy tropical rainstorm. Within hours the Spanish retreated behind the walls of Intramuros and then surrendered. The Americans suffered 17 killed and 105 wounded. Three days later, news arrived that an armistice had already been signed, but the information had been delayed because the U.S. Navy had cut the undersea telegraph cable during its initial attack. *(Map 1)*

The United States now controlled Manila but not the countryside. Merritt and Dewey telegraphed Washington for instructions on how to treat the Filipino insurgents. The War Department replied that there would be no joint occupation of Manila and that the insurgents "must recognize the military occupation and authority of the United States." The Army was given the task of establishing control over this distant land, if necessary against armed opposition.

Less well understood at the time was that the United States had been catapulted into a region on the verge of profound crisis, torn by instability and great power rivalry. The Manchu dynasty in China was faltering, while Japan was emerging as Asia's first modern power and acquiring an empire of its own. Britain, France, and the Netherlands were determined to hold on to their existing empires. As the new century unfolded, America was no longer an outside observer but part of the regional great power system with possessions and expanding commercial interests to protect. The U.S. Army was inexorably drawn into this unfamiliar arena of conflict.

Philippine nationalists declared their independence, but the United States refused to recognize this. The VIII Corps, sent to capture Manila from the Spanish, awaited further instructions. Merritt left to join the American peace delegation in Paris, leaving Maj. Gen. Elwell S. Otis in command. The American soldiers held defensive lines around Manila for almost six months as the *Filipino Army of Liberation* camped outside, both sides waiting for the peace negotiations. In December, the United States and Spain signed the Treaty of Paris, which gave independence to Cuba but not to the Philippines. The treaty gave the Philippines to the United States in exchange for a $20-million payment to Spain. President McKinley ordered the Army to extend military government "with all possible dispatch to the whole of the ceded territory" and to demonstrate that "the mission of the United States is one of benevolent assimilation, substituting the mild sway of justice and right for arbitrary rule." The insurrectionists felt betrayed. On the night of 4–5 February 1899, patrols clashed in the dark and Otis launched an offensive to push the rebels away from the capital. It took only a few weeks to defeat the revolutionary army and capture the provisional rebel capital, but the rebels refused to accept defeat.

The Army now faced a protracted campaign that required more manpower. The state volunteers had enlisted for the duration of the War with Spain, which was now over. In 1899, Congress authorized a temporary force of U.S. Volunteers specifically for service in the Philippines. These fresh soldiers began to arrive in September, augmented by state volunteers who were enticed to stay in the Philippines by a large enlistment bonus. The U.S. Volunteers increased American troop strength to almost twenty-seven thousand, which enabled the VIII Corps to push into northern Luzon. In November, Aguinaldo ordered the remnants of his army to shift from conventional to guerrilla warfare.

The Army now fought to extend its authority throughout the archipelago in a small-unit war, similar in many ways to the Army's frontier campaigns against the Indians. Most senior officers and noncommissioned officers brought with them the skills and experiences of that kind of fighting. The VIII Corps created regional commands and posted detachments around the country, which gave great autonomy to small-unit leaders. The guerrillas knew they could not defeat the Americans outright, so

Troops fording a river in the Philippines, 1899

instead fought to inflict losses that would cause the Americans to abandon their objectives. American soldiers struggled against boredom, climate, fatigue, and tropical diseases. They learned to call their rations by a pidgin word, "chow." They endured endless patrols through the "boondocks," the Tagalog word for "mountain." They could never be sure that civilians did not support the insurgents, and sometimes called them derogatory names such as "goo-goo" or "gook."

In the fall of 1899, the Army began to organize small indigenous units, called Philippine Scouts, under the leadership of American officers. The Scouts provided essential language and cultural skills and proved effective in suppressing the guerrillas. In 1901, Congress authorized the Philippine Scouts as part of the U.S. Army.

The United States had no government agency responsible for governing overseas possessions, so the War Department was given the job. In December 1898, it established a Division of Customs and Insular Affairs (renamed the Bureau of Insular Affairs in 1902). In the Philippines, U.S. soldiers built schools, roads, bridges, and railroads and implemented modern public health measures to encourage pacification. In July 1901, the

9

Soldiers mingle with Filipinos.

Army helped organize the Philippine Constabulary as one historian later called a "police force to control brigandage and deal with the remnants of the insurgent movement." Army troop strength reached some seventy thousand, which enabled the Army to wage simultaneous campaigns in different areas. The Navy provided mobility and fire support throughout the archipelago and restricted the guerrillas from moving among the islands. The Army used a carrot-and-stick approach, combining harsh coercive measures, such as burning crops and buildings of troublesome areas, with conciliation and civic action. In some areas, the Army "concentrated" the civilian population to separate them from the guerrillas, a tactic that had outraged the American public when the Spanish did the same in Cuba.

The American public grew uneasy with its new empire. In February 1899, British author Rudyard Kipling urged America to take up "the white man's burden," but many Americans disagreed. During the 1900 presidential campaign, Democratic Party candidate William Jennings Bryan denounced America's involvement. Fighters on both sides committed atrocities, which were widely reported in American newspapers. In September 1901, Filipinos surprised an American unit in Balangiga on Samar and killed more than forty soldiers. The Army retaliated brutally, killing large numbers of civilians as well as insurgents. When American military authorities court-martialed soldiers accused of atrocities, the trials fed the flames of controversy at home.

In March 1900, President McKinley appointed William H. Taft to chair a commission to organize a civilian government, and in July 1901, the United States established civilian rule over much of the Philippines. Taft became the first civilian governor-general. Army officers worked closely with American and Filipino civilian officials toward the mutual goal of restoring law, order, and administration to the Philippines. The commission continued the Army's nation-building activities. For example, in 1901–1902 the commission recruited more than one thousand American civilian teachers from the United States. The first group was carried to the Philippines aboard the U.S. Army Transport *Thomas*, so they were nicknamed "Thomasites." America's first overseas colony became America's first major nation-building project.

The Army gradually subdued the insurgents with a judicious mix of attraction and chastisement. In March 1901, Brig. Gen. Frederick N. Funston used an elaborate ruse to capture Aguinaldo. Although much hard fighting remained in southern Luzon and Samar, the Army broke the insurrection by the end of the year. The U.S. Volunteers mustered out that summer, leaving the last fighting to the regulars and a marine battalion, which participated in the campaign on Samar in 1901–1902. On 4 July 1902, President Theodore Roosevelt declared the unpopular war over. The war cost the Army about four thousand deaths, three thousand of which died from disease. As one measure of the intensity of the fighting, seventy soldiers were awarded the Medal of Honor.

Active service in the Philippines marked a generation of Army leaders. Every Army chief of staff from 1903 through General George C. Marshall served in the Philippines, some more than once. Taft returned to Washington in 1904 to become secretary of war and was elected president in 1908. In 1913, veterans of the War with Spain and the Philippine Insurrection formed the Veterans of Foreign Wars. The Army's experiences in the region left a permanent mark on the institution and the soldiers who served there.

PACIFIC OUTPOSTS, 1900–1937

Once the United States became part of the international system in the Far East, it used the Army to protect the country's interests. Japan was modernizing rapidly and asserting itself as a regional power. China was suffering from internal instability and was unable to defend itself against outside forces. France, Britain, Germany, and the Netherlands kept a tight grip on their possessions in South and Southeast Asia against the rising force of nationalism. Technology was transforming the region, including steam ships, railroads, petroleum, telegraphy, radio, and aviation.

China's descent into chaos became the key challenge, and conditions grew worse after its humiliating defeat at the hands of Japan in 1894–1895. The United States declared an "open door" policy to prevent China from being carved into spheres of influence, which became the foundation of American policy in Asia until 1941. As the Chinese government attempted reforms, a popular movement, the "Boxers," arose to drive out foreign influences. In 1900, the Boxers laid siege to the foreign legations in Peking (Beijing) and attacked foreign-operated railroads. As a result, Japan, Russia, France, Britain, and the United States deployed an international peacekeeping force. This became the Army's first experience in coalition operations since the American Revolution.

In July 1900, the Army joined the China Relief Expedition under Japanese command to attack the port of Tientsin (Tianjin), the gateway to Peking. The Army sent two regiments from the Philippines and one from the United States. Maj. Gen. Adna R. Chaffee, a veteran of the Civil War and Indian Wars, commanded the contingent of twenty-five hundred American soldiers and marines that marched with the international force seventy miles to Peking in temperatures exceeding 100°F, then fought a sharp battle to end the 55-day siege of the legation quarter. For several months afterward, the international forces administered the city and sent expeditions into the surrounding countryside to root out the last vestiges of Boxer resistance. Chaffee returned to the Philippines and was promoted to Army chief of staff in 1904.

In the Philippines, the Army continued to fight bandits for several years, aided by the Philippine Constabulary and Philippine Scout companies. In the southern islands, the Army confronted a different kind of resistance. On the islands of Mindanao, Sulu, and

12

other smaller islands was a Muslim society quite different from that of the Christianized north, a society of Muslim tribesmen known as Moros. As had the Spanish before them, American commanders used a mix of persuasion and coercion to subdue the Moros. In 1899, Brig. Gen. John C. Bates negotiated an agreement with the sultan of Sulu by which the sultan recognized U.S. sovereignty, while the United States agreed to pay him an annuity, to respect his jurisdiction in criminal cases involving only Muslims, and to respect local religious customs. In November 1901, Capt. John J. Pershing led a force to subdue the *datos* (tribal chiefs) and their tribesmen. When Maj. Gen. Leonard Wood became governor of the Moro Province in 1903, he attempted even harsher measures. When Pershing returned in 1909 as a brigadier general and governor of Mindanao, he found the situation improved, but armed resistance continued until 1913.

In 1904–1905, the regional strategic situation changed dramatically. Japan's empire already included Taiwan, the Ryukyus, and Korea. In February 1904, Japan began a war with Russia with a surprise naval attack against the Russian fleet at Port Arthur in Manchuria. The U.S. Army sent a handful of officers, including Captain Pershing, to observe the land campaign. When Japan defeated Russia, the United States realized it could not leave its possessions undefended against this rising power and developed a joint Army-Navy contingency plan for war against Japan, War Plan ORANGE. As the Philippine Commission assumed more governmental functions, including policing with the Philippine Constabulary, the Army turned its attention to external defense.

In Hawaii and the Philippines, the Army built coastal defenses and permanent posts. In Hawaii, these building projects included Fort Shafter and Schofield Barracks and coast artillery batteries at Fort DeRussy and elsewhere on Oahu. Meanwhile, the Army Corps of Engineers built civil works, including harbors and lighthouses, and dredged the entrance to Pearl Harbor.

Near Manila, Army engineers built Fort William McKinley, named after the president who first sent soldiers to the islands. This 8,045-acre post became home to the Philippine Division headquarters. Eighty miles further north and with a higher elevation and healthier climate, the Army built Fort Stotsenburg on some 151,000 acres, which became home to field artillery and cavalry units. A lieutenant with the 5th Field Artillery wrote a song in 1908 about field training at the post that was later set to music by

John Philip Sousa and made into the Army song: "Over hill, over dale, we have hit the dusty trail, / As the caissons go rolling along."

After a war scare with Japan in 1907, the Army also built modern coast artillery fortifications to defend Manila and Subic Bay. At the mouth of Manila Bay, Fort Mills on Corregidor Island became an island fortress. Philippine Scout units were trained in coastal defense to augment the limited American units. The Army also opened the U.S. Military Academy to promising Filipino cadets. The first graduate was Vincente Lim, class of 1914, who later rose to chief of staff of the Philippine Army. Over the next quarter century, more than twenty Filipinos graduated from the academy, going on to lead the Philippine Scouts and later the Philippine Army.

The War Department's poor experience with commercial shipping during the War with Spain led it to create the Army Transport Service to operate a small fleet of vessels in the region. The War Department found it prudent in war and peace to have its own vessels for overseas movement of soldiers, horses, and materiel.

After the Klondike gold rush, the War Department did not regularly station units in Alaska. However, from 1900 to 1904, the Signal Corps built the Washington-Alaska Military Cable and Telegraph System to connect the populated sections of the territory with the Pacific Northwest with a network that included 1,497 miles of land lines, 2,128 miles of submarine cable, and a wireless link of 107 miles.

The War Department gradually put its overseas garrisons on a more permanent basis. It organized the Hawaiian Department in 1911 and the Philippine Department in 1913. The Corps of Engineers completed the Panama Canal in 1914, linking the Atlantic and Pacific. The Army also built and manned modern coast artillery defenses for Manila, Honolulu, and the West Coast ports. But with the outbreak of war in Europe, the War Department stripped these two departments of most of their regular units and personnel. In the Philippines, the Army left behind the 31st Infantry and organized the Philippine Scout companies into five provisional regiments. In Hawaii, the War Department called up the Hawaii National Guard.

The Great War had little direct impact in the Far East, but Japan declared war on Germany and seized Germany's possessions in China and the Pacific, including the Mariana, Caroline, and Marshall Islands, which complicated the U.S. Navy's war planning.

14

Artillerymen firing a 12-inch disappearing gun at Battery Selfridge in the 1920s. Once part of the harbor defenses of Oahu, Battery Selfridge is now on Joint Base Pearl Harbor-Hickam.

Australia and New Zealand took German New Guinea, the Bismarck Archipelago, and the Solomon Islands. After the war at the Washington naval disarmament talks, the United States agreed to tonnage limits and not to further fortify its possessions in the western Pacific. The Army continued to man the coastal defenses of Manila and Honolulu, but construction and improvements ceased. The Philippine Department organized fifteen Philippine Scout (PS) coast artillery companies, which were reorganized in 1924 into the 91st and 92d Coast Artillery (PS), alongside two regular U.S. coast artillery regiments.

In 1918, when the Russian Bolshevik revolutionaries signed a separate peace with Germany, Japan organized a coalition to intervene in Siberia, the Russian Far East. Along with Japan, Britain, and France, the United States contributed nine thousand soldiers, including the 31st Infantry from the Philippines and others from the 8th Division at Camp Fremont, California, which had been only weeks away from movement to France. The secretary of war summoned the division commander, Maj. Gen. William S. Graves, and handed him President Woodrow Wilson's instructions: "This contains the policy of the

15

United States in Russia which you are to follow. Watch your step; you will be walking on eggs loaded with dynamite."

The American Expeditionary Forces, Siberia, arrived in Vladivostok in August and September 1918 and were soon patrolling the railroad all the way to Lake Baikal. General Graves struggled to remain neutral in the complex situation with monarchist White Russians, Red Communist partisans, anti-Communist Cossacks, former Austro-Hungarian prisoners of war organized as the Czech Legion, and other international contingents, the largest being the Imperial Japanese Army with seventy thousand troops. Eventually, the United States agreed to transport the Czech Legion to Trieste and Fiume in the Adriatic Sea aboard eleven U.S. Army transports. The American contingent was withdrawn in April 1920. Graves' chief intelligence officer, Lt. Col. Robert L. Eichelberger, saw harbingers of future trouble. "When I departed the Japanese were in full control of eastern Siberia," he later wrote. "Out of my Siberian experiences came a conviction that pursued me for the next twenty years: I knew that Japanese militarism had as its firm purpose the conquest of all Asia." The Bolsheviks consolidated their control over the Russian Far East in 1922.

In the 1920s, after more than twenty tumultuous years, the Army settled into a peacetime routine. In 1921, the War Department organized the Hawaiian Division and the Philippine Division. For the next two decades these two divisions, with organic infantry, cavalry, field artillery, and supporting arms, were the largest combined arms formations in the Army. A generation of officers and noncommissioned officers learned to soldier in the region. Stationed in the Philippines was the "Carabao Army," consisting of about five thousand American soldiers with about sixty-five hundred Philippine Scouts. The Americans usually served overseas for three-year tours. Officers often brought their families, while enlisted men sometimes married local women. The units would conduct large-scale maneuvers every year to train for the defense of Luzon. With the insurrection fading into memory, the Philippine Scouts evolved into well-trained garrison units under the direction of American officers. The Army organized the Philippine Scouts into permanent regiments, including the 45th and 57th Infantry (PS), 24th Field Artillery (PS), and supporting arms. When the 9th Cavalry, the last African American unit stationed in the Philippines, returned to the United States in 1922, it left its vehicles, horses, and equipment to the 26th Cavalry (PS).

But pay for the Philippine Scouts was about one-third what their American counterparts received, which led to a brief mutiny in 1924 at Fort William McKinley.

Army units in the Philippines supported contingency operations in the region, including humanitarian assistance. On 1 September 1923, a powerful earthquake struck the Tokyo area, killing over one hundred thousand people. Within a week, the Philippine Department shipped over sixteen thousand tons of subsistence stores, tentage, clothing, and medical supplies to the stricken city.

During the 1920s, America's policy towards the Philippines remained unclear, but in 1934, Congress called for complete independence after a ten-year transition. Until then, the United States would retain responsibility for its defense. The Philippine Senate requested an American military mission to begin building its own defense capabilities. The Philippine president-elect, Manuel L. Quezon, invited the retiring Chief of Staff of the Army, General Douglas MacArthur, who had served three previous tours in the Philippines, to serve as his military adviser. MacArthur brought his personal staff, including his aide, Maj. Dwight D. Eisenhower. Together, they set about building a new army for the Philippine Commonwealth.

In China, the 15th Infantry was stationed in Tientsin to protect American citizens and serve as part of an international force to keep open the rail lines to Peking, alongside British, French, Italian, and Japanese troops. This regiment was the Army's showcase unit in the region because of its high professional standards and rigorous training. It had first been posted there in 1912 when Chinese revolutionaries established the Chinese Republic. International forces remained during the civil war and anarchy of the 1920s and 1930s. When Col. George C. Marshall served as regimental executive officer from 1924 to 1927, rival warlords often threatened the international settlement but never attacked the Americans. In one such incident, a force of about twelve thousand Chinese soldiers approached Tientsin, and Maj. Matthew B. Ridgway went out on horseback with two other soldiers to meet them and watch them turn away. The commander of U.S. forces in China recommended that these forces be withdrawn, as they could do little to help stabilize the country and were too few to defend themselves, commenting that: "During the recent war we escaped conflict by as narrow a margin as I consider possible." Elsewhere in

Soldiers of the 31st Infantry defend the perimeter of Shanghai's foreign quarter in March 1932.

China, the 4th Marines were posted in Shanghai in 1927 and Navy gunboats patrolled the Yangtze River.

In 1932, Japan landed seventy thousand soldiers in Shanghai to battle Chinese warlords for control of southern China. The U.S. Army chief of staff sent an urgent cable to the Philippine Department to deploy the 31st Infantry "to furnish protection for American lives and property in International Settlement. . . . Equip troops for indefinite stay and every emergency. Leave animals behind for present." The regiment sailed for Shanghai with a company of marines to reinforce the 4th Marines alongside other European forces. According to one historian: "The troops served as a neutral force, protecting foreign lives and property. . . . Operating under strict rules of engagement, the infantrymen endeavored to achieve their objectives through tact, conciliation, and intimidation rather than by force. In this they were successful." After several tense months, the soldiers withdrew.

In Hawaii, soldiers called themselves the "Pineapple Army." Most of the fifteen thousand soldiers were stationed on the island of Oahu at Schofield Barracks. The Army and Navy conducted exercises every year or two in and around the Hawaiian Islands, funding permitting. Hawaii, the linchpin of America's defenses in the region, became known as the Gibraltar of the Pacific. The soldiers would rehearse defeating beach landings and air raids. In 1921, the War Department formally established a Reserve Officers' Training Corps at the University of Hawaii, as well as the National Guard and Organized Reserve Corps. In 1933, when President Franklin D. Roosevelt established the Civilian Conservation Corps, the Hawaiian Department established camps where young men were put to work on public works projects under the direction of Army officers and noncommissioned officers.

In Alaska, the War Department stationed small elements of the 7th Infantry at Chilkoot Barracks in Haines, which had been an important supply center for the Klondike gold rush. The University of Alaska in Fairbanks established a Reserve Officers' Training Corps in 1936. But this relative neglect of Alaska's defenses was changing with the growth of long-range commercial and military aviation. In November 1935, Pan American Airways sent the *China Clipper*, a flying boat that could carry thirty-six passengers, on the first commercial flight from San Francisco to Manila by way of Honolulu, Midway, Wake, and Guam. But Alaska and the remote Aleutian Islands were the shortest air route to Northeast Asia. In 1934, former Army Air Corps Brig. Gen. Billy Mitchell declared that "in the future he who holds Alaska will rule the world."

THE GATHERING STORM, 1937–1941

By 1937, the era of peacetime soldiering and small-scale contingency operations in the Far East was coming to an end. In July, the Imperial Japanese Army began a full-scale invasion of China. In December, Japanese planes attacked a U.S. Navy gunboat, the USS *Panay*, on the Yangtze River near Nanking. The United States realized the seriousness of the situation and withdrew the 15th Infantry from Tientsin. In 1939, when another world war erupted in Europe, the great power rivalry in the Far East threatened to explode as Japan sought to create a Greater East Asia Co-prosperity Sphere. The War Department reassessed its plans and posture and reviewed War Plan ORANGE, but the mismatch between the threat and available resources could not be reconciled. British and American planners had already agreed that, if the United States became involved in the war, its priority would be the defeat of Germany, not Japan.

The Philippine Department focused on the defense of Manila Bay, including the island fortress of Corregidor, while MacArthur's military mission hurried to create the Philippine Army. Military dependents in the Philippines were sent back to the United States in June 1941. In July, the War Department activated a new command, the U.S. Army Forces in the Far East, and called "the organized forces of the Government of the Commonwealth of the Philippines" into the service of the United States, under MacArthur's command. In August, the War Department sent National Guard units to the Philippines, including the 200th Coast Artillery (Anti-Aircraft), the 192d and 194th Tank Battalions, along with aircraft, ammunition and supplies, and hundreds of reserve officers. The Navy sent reinforcements, including submarines. The Philippine Scouts doubled to twelve thousand. In September, elements of the Philippine Army were mobilized. Each new Philippine division was assigned forty U.S. officers and twenty noncommissioned officers as instructors. A senior American adviser told a new instructor: "You have no command status. You have no authority. But you are directly responsible for the success or failure of the regiment." MacArthur expected that his command would be ready for war by April 1942.

In 1940, the War Department began to reinforce Alaska and organized the Alaska National Guard. That June, the Army Corps of Engineers began construction of several air bases and a large base near Anchorage, Fort Richardson, named for Brig. Gen. Wilds P. Richardson, who had served three tours of duty in Alaska between 1897 and 1917. The Navy also built up its forces in Alaskan waters. In February 1941, the War Department created the Alaska Defense Command. By December 1941, Army ground forces in Alaska had grown from a few hundred to about twenty thousand, including four infantry regiments, three-and-a-half antiaircraft regiments, and supporting troops.

The Hawaiian Department also mobilized for war. The Pacific Fleet had shifted from San Diego to Pearl Harbor in the spring of 1940, adding the defense of the fleet to the Army's mission set. That fall, the National Guard was called to active duty, and Selective Service put several thousand young men into training at Schofield Barracks. Unlike regular soldiers, the selectees reflected Hawaii's unique racial mixture, including more than two thousand American citizens of Japanese ancestry. The Army Corps of Engineers improved defenses, built underground gasoline and ammunition storage facilities, and worked on hundreds of other construction projects, including an air ferry route from Hawaii to Australia along a string of remote South Pacific islands to bypass Japanese-controlled islands. The Signal Corps began testing an experimental new technology, radar. In February 1941, Lt. Gen. Walter C. Short arrived to bring the Hawaiian Department to wartime readiness. That fall, the Hawaiian Department organized the 24th and 25th Infantry Divisions. National Guard units and individual replacements poured in from the United States, bringing Army manpower in Hawaii to over forty-three thousand, most stationed on Oahu. In late November, after the conclusion of extensive field maneuvers, the Hawaiian Department received word from the War Department that diplomatic talks with Japan appeared to be terminated: "Prior to hostile Japanese action, you are directed to undertake such reconnaissance and other measures as you deem necessary but these measures should be carried out so as not, repeat not, to alarm the civil population or disclose intent." General Short ordered his command to prepare for possible sabotage or internal unrest, and awaited further developments.

PACIFIC WAR AND AFTERMATH 1941–1950

THE THIN RED LINE, 1941–1943

World War II began with two crushing defeats for the U.S. Army. In Hawaii on 7 December 1941, the Army failed to defend the vaunted Gibraltar of the Pacific against a surprise air raid by the Japanese Navy, despite having two infantry divisions and four antiaircraft regiments stationed in the territory. The novelist James Jones, who was then a soldier at Schofield Barracks, later told how a cynical Regular Army first sergeant growled to his panicked soldiers: "All right, all right you men. Quiet down. Quiet down. Its only a war. Aint you never been in a war before?" The soldiers would see enough of war in the coming years, but the senior Army and Navy commanders in Hawaii who had permitted the defeat were relieved at once. *(Map 2)*

In the Philippines, long the keystone of the Army's regional defenses, a Japanese air raid the same day destroyed the Far East Air Force on the ground, ending any chance of an effective defense against a Japanese invasion. General MacArthur organized his forces to defend Luzon; but with little air cover or hope of reinforcement, defeat was a matter of time. The Japanese Army landed on 22 December. MacArthur conducted a delaying action, then declared Manila an open city and shifted his forces to the jungle-covered Bataan Peninsula. There the Philippine and American forces fought

23

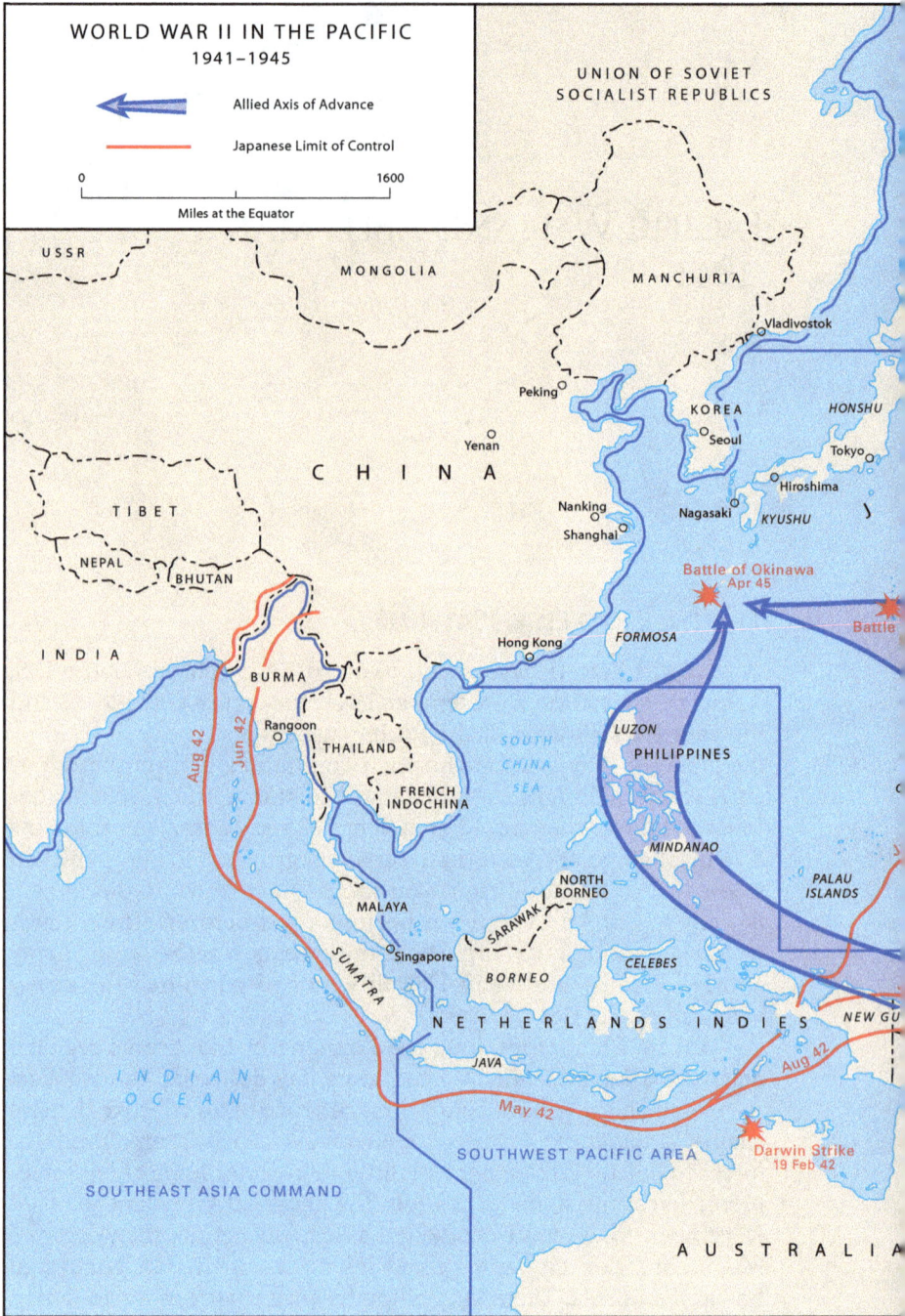

WORLD WAR II IN THE PACIFIC
1941–1945

Allied Axis of Advance

Japanese Limit of Control

0   1600
Miles at the Equator

UNION OF SOVIET
SOCIALIST REPUBLICS

USSR

MONGOLIA

MANCHURIA

Vladivostok

Peking

KOREA   HONSHU

Seoul

Yenan   Tokyo

CHINA

Hiroshima

Nanking   Nagasaki   KYUSHU

Shanghai

TIBET

NEPAL
BHUTAN

Battle of Okinawa
Apr 45

Hong Kong   FORMOSA   Battle

INDIA

BURMA

Aug 42   Jun 42   Rangoon

THAILAND

FRENCH
INDOCHINA

SOUTH
CHINA
SEA

LUZON

PHILIPPINES

MINDANAO

PALAU
ISLANDS

MALAYA

Singapore

SARAWAK

NORTH
BORNEO

CELEBES

SUMATRA

BORNEO

NETHERLANDS   INDIES   NEW GU

Aug 42

INDIAN
OCEAN

JAVA

May 42

SOUTHWEST PACIFIC AREA

Darwin Strike
19 Feb 42

SOUTHEAST ASIA COMMAND

AUSTRALIA

Map 2

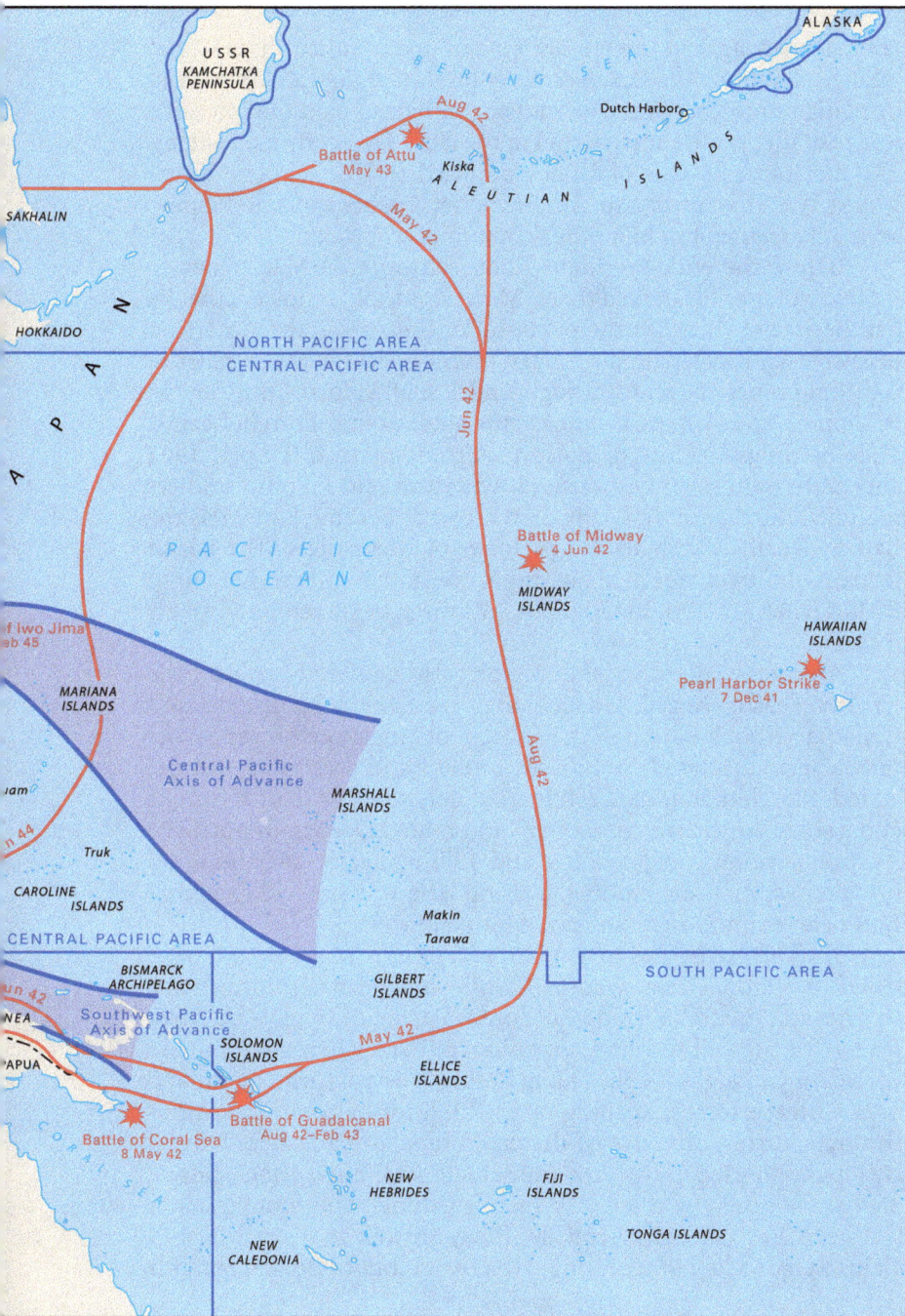

courageously against the enemy, terrain and weather, disease, and finally starvation. The Japanese Navy prevented the U.S. Navy from bringing reinforcements. The soldiers on Bataan paid the price of a war plan that was doomed to fail in the face of a determined enemy. The first three Medals of Honor awarded to U.S. soldiers during World War II went to two American lieutenants and one Filipino sergeant assigned to Philippine Scout units on Bataan.

Before the end, President Roosevelt ordered MacArthur to Australia. Once he arrived there, MacArthur told reporters that he had been sent there for the purpose "of organizing the American offensive against Japan, a primary object of which is the relief of the Philippines. I came through and I shall return." But for the Philippine and American forces still holding out, no relief came. The "battling bastards of Bataan" surrendered on 9 April 1942 and more than seventy thousand American and Filipino soldiers marched into captivity. Many died on what became known as the Bataan Death March to the prisoner-of-war camps. The island fortress of Corregidor held out under constant bombardment until 6 May, when Lt. Gen. Jonathan M. Wainwright surrendered all his forces.

America's allies in the region also suffered defeat. The Japanese easily seized Hong Kong, garrisoned by British and Canadian troops; captured the fortress of Singapore on the Straits of Malacca, defended by British, Indian, and Australian troops; seized the Netherlands East Indies, defended by Dutch troops and a small American contingent; and raided Darwin in northern Australia, sinking eight ships and killing nearly two hundred fifty people. In a few months, a rising Asian power had shattered European empires that had stood for centuries.

The U.S. Army had to respond everywhere at once. The Army Chief of Staff, General George C. Marshall, sent reinforcements to Hawaii, Australia, and the South Pacific. He sent Lt. Gen. Joseph W. Stilwell to serve as senior military adviser to Chinese President Chiang Kai-shek (Jiǎng Jièshí), who gave him command over Chinese forces, keeping open the lines of communications through Burma. Because of the rapid Japanese advance, Stilwell was lucky to escape with his immediate staff amid thousands of civilian refugees by a ten-day march through the mountains of northern Burma. On arrival in India, Stilwell told reporters: "I claim we got a hell of a beating. We got run out of Burma and it is humiliating as hell. I think we ought to find out what caused it, go back and retake the place."

In the face of these defeats, the Hawaiian Department braced for an invasion and declared martial law. Thirty thousand military dependents were evacuated to the mainland. Years of racial prejudice and plantation labor strife had made Army officials wary of the large Japanese population. As soon as the first reinforcements arrived from the mainland, the Hawaiian Department sent thirteen hundred second-generation Japanese American soldiers to the mainland. These *Nisei* were organized into the 100th Infantry Battalion (Separate) and later fought valiantly in Italy and France. Hawaii became the springboard to victory as millions of soldiers, sailors, airmen, and marines poured through, along with millions of tons of war materiel. On the mainland, the Western Defense Command declared the entire West Coast a military restricted area and ordered the removal of more than a hundred thousand persons of Japanese ancestry.

The Japanese, instead of attacking Hawaii, raided the American naval base at Dutch Harbor in the Aleutian Islands in June and landed detachments on Attu and Kiska. At Midway in the Central Pacific, the Japanese fleet met decisive defeat at the hands of the U.S. Navy and Army Air Forces.

During the first year, the Army scrambled to establish new bases of operations in Australia and New Zealand, both of which had been left exposed when the British government sent their armed forces to the Middle East. The United States created air and sea lines of communications via Tonga, Efate in the New Hebrides, Fiji, and French New Caledonia. The War Department rushed two National Guard divisions to Australia, and in September, MacArthur airlifted two regiments into Papua New Guinea to fight alongside the Australian Army in some of the most forbidding terrain in the world. When the American infantry bogged down near Buna, MacArthur ordered the I Corps commander, Lt. Gen. Robert L. Eichelberger, to take personal command. After months of combat, the Americans and Australians finally defeated the Japanese by 22 January 1943. This ended the immediate threat of an invasion of Australia, but at a cost of 8,546 Allied killed and wounded. It took almost a year to reconstitute the 32d Infantry Division.

Nine hundred miles to the east of New Guinea, Japan seized the Solomon Islands to threaten the lifeline to Australia.

Men of the 31st Infantry Division cross a river near Saidor on New Guinea, January 1944.

On 7 August 1942, the Navy responded by landing the 1st Marine Division to capture a Japanese airfield under construction on Guadalcanal. The United States eventually reinforced with two Army divisions, another Marine division, and an Army corps headquarters, supported by air and naval forces, which together pressed home a costly victory by February 1943. These soldiers and marines formed the "thin red line" that halted the Japanese advance. After the American victory, General Marshall reassigned two key leaders to Europe to share their hard-won experience in amphibious and joint operations: XIV Corps commanding general, Maj. Gen. Alexander M. Patch, and 25th Infantry Division commanding general, Maj. Gen. J. Lawton Collins. Both men rose to higher command.

Behind the battlefront, Army quartermasters, engineers, signaleers, transporters, and medical personnel built up the joint theater logistics infrastructure essential to victory in the air, on land, and on sea. In the spring of 1942, Chief of Naval Operations Admiral Ernest J. King was rumored to have said, "I don't know what the hell this 'logistics' is that Marshall is always talking about, but I want some of it."

Across the region, soldiers repeatedly proved their ability to adapt and innovate in every imaginable environment. Soldiers learned to fight the close fight and prevail against a tenacious enemy. Small-unit leadership was key to mission accomplishment in amphibious assaults, jungle fighting, infantry-tank cooperation, and fire support. In the process, soldiers developed an intense hatred of their Japanese opponents, inspired by combat fury and a deep-rooted anti-Japanese prejudice common in prewar America. With "Remember Pearl Harbor!" as the country's rallying cry, the conflict became what historian John W. Dower has described as a "war without mercy."

The Army Ground Forces learned to work closely with the Army Air Forces, Navy, and Marine Corps. In particular, amphibious operations required close coordination. Theater commanders often organized joint task forces for specific operations. In the Southwest Pacific, MacArthur's command included the Sixth Army, Fifth Air Force, and Seventh Fleet, as well as Australian forces. Soldiers usually fought in regimental combat teams that combined infantry, field artillery, engineer, and support units.

As the scale of operations grew, corps- and army-level headquarters became important for command and control. On Guadalcanal, an Army corps headquarters commanded Army and Marine units. The Southwest Pacific Area started with one field army and one corps; by 1944, it had grown to two field armies and four corps. The South Pacific Area and Central Pacific Area each used one Army corps. For Okinawa, the War Department activated the Tenth Army to command the Army's XXIV Corps and the III Marine Amphibious Corps. By the end of the war, soldiers outnumbered marines in the Pacific by more than three to one, not counting the Army Air Forces. The Marine Corps provided two amphibious corps and six divisions; the Army provided three field armies, six corps, twenty-one divisions, and logistical support to several theaters. In all, the Army made more amphibious landings in the Pacific than the Marine Corps.

The Army also worked closely with Allies. In the Philippines, it had fought alongside the Philippine Army and small numbers of Army officers later organized Philippine guerrilla bands against the Japanese occupying forces. In New Guinea, it fought with Australians. In the Solomon Islands, it fought with New Zealanders. In Alaska and the Aleutian Islands, it fought with Canadians, including the combined U.S.-Canadian First Special Service Force. In Burma, it fought with British, Commonwealth, and Chinese units.

The war in the Pacific saw technology develop at a rapid pace. Before Pearl Harbor, the War Department fielded the new M1 Garand rifle in the Philippines and Hawaii, and it performed exceptionally well. The Chemical Warfare Service fielded the man-portable flamethrower, which proved effective against bunkers and caves. Because Japan was rumored to have used chemical weapons in China before 1941, the Army maintained readiness to retaliate in kind and stockpiled hundreds of tons of chemical munitions in Australia and Hawaii. The Army developed the capability to make

Soldiers of the 7th Infantry Division attack a Japanese position with a flamethrower on Kwajalein Island, 4 February 1944.

opposed amphibious landings, building on Marine Corps doctrinal development before the war. Soldiers learned to handle Higgins boats and amphibious tractors, which were essential for crossing coral reefs. The Army created six engineer special brigades for amphibious landings, four of which served in the Pacific. MacArthur also used airborne units, including the 503d Parachute Infantry in New Guinea and the 11th Airborne Division on Luzon.

Fire support for amphibious operations was unusually complex. For a successful landing, the orchestration of air and naval bombardment was critical. Once soldiers came ashore, organic field artillery and mortars were added. Major operations later in the war saw the employment of field artillery on an unprecedented scale, sometimes directed by air observation posts.

The Signal Corps faced unprecedented challenges to link together communications networks over half the globe. For amphibious operations, Army signaleers invented a new tactical signal organization, the Joint Assault Signal Company.

On islands devoid of modern infrastructure, Army engineers built entire cities, ports, roads, bridges, petroleum pipelines, water systems, electrical systems, and airfields. MacArthur stated the obvious when he said, "This is an air and amphibious war; because of the nature of air and amphibious operations, it is distinctly an engineer's war."

For the first time the Army fielded extensive intelligence capabilities throughout the region. Each regiment had an intelligence and reconnaissance platoon; divisions and corps had intelligence sections. Senior intelligence officers built large organizations for translation, interrogation, order of battle, technical intelligence, and signals intelligence at the theater level. In Brisbane, Central Bureau employed over one thousand American and Australian personnel, who used the latest IBM collators, tabulators, and printers to decipher Japanese message traffic. In Hawaii, the J–2, an Army engineer officer, created the Joint Intelligence Center, Pacific Ocean Areas, an innovative all-source intelligence center with nearly eighteen hundred Army and Navy personnel. The Army used several thousand Japanese American soldiers as translators and interpreters down to the regimental level.

The Medical Corps treated tropical diseases in the South Pacific and frostbite in the Aleutians. Army medicine made great strides in protecting soldiers against malaria and other tropical diseases and pioneered aerial evacuation. Despite the challenges of time and distance, the Army medical system provided unparalleled care.

African American soldiers served in the Pacific, but in segregated units. The 24th and 25th Infantry regiments fought in the Solomon Islands and New Guinea. Twelve thousand black soldiers served in antiaircraft units. The first Distinguished Service Cross for an African American in World War II was awarded to Pvt. George Watson of the 29th Quartermaster, who lost his life in March 1943 while rescuing fellow soldiers from a sinking ship that had been attacked by enemy bombers near New Guinea. More than four thousand five hundred black soldiers served in more than twenty-five amphibian truck companies in support of dozens of assault landings, including Iwo Jima and Okinawa. About one hundred thousand black soldiers served in the Pacific and more than twenty thousand in China-Burma-India, where over half of the Americans building the Ledo Road were African American.

Thousands of women served in the Pacific in the Army Nurse Corps or Women's Army Corps. Before the war, over a hundred nurses were assigned to the Philippines; sixty-seven became prisoners of war. Others served in Hawaii, Alaska, and the Southwest Pacific. In July 1944, the War Department sent about four hundred to China-Burma-India to serve with the Army Air Forces.

As Army and Navy commanders parried Japanese thrusts in 1942–1943, the Joint Chiefs of Staff hammered out a strategy. They established two independent theaters: the Southwest Pacific Area under General MacArthur, based in Australia, and the Pacific Ocean Areas under Admiral Chester W. Nimitz, based in Hawaii. Nimitz also created a subordinate command, the South Pacific Area, headquartered in the French colony of New Caledonia until the Solomons campaign concluded in 1944. American prewar plans had not envisioned two separate theaters, but the loss of the Philippines, coupled with Roosevelt's desire to give MacArthur a command appropriate to his stature, made two theaters inevitable. In the Central Pacific, closely supervised by the chief of naval operations, Nimitz followed the general lines of War Plan ORANGE as it had been repeatedly rehearsed during the interwar period, while also clearing the Solomon Islands. In the Southwest Pacific, American and Australian soldiers fought on the world's second largest island, New Guinea, and the Bismarck Archipelago, before turning north toward the Philippines. The struggle for resources between competing theaters made interservice rivalry inevitable, forcing the Army chief of staff "to become deeply involved in interservice quarrels and special problems," according to Forrest C. Pogue, General Marshall's biographer, and "to serve as a buffer between the Army and Navy leaders in the Pacific, helping to provide a measure of unity that would otherwise have been lacking."

In 1944, the Joint Chiefs of Staff added a third line of operations, strategic bombardment of Japan with the Boeing B–29 Superfortress, by the Twentieth Air Force, which reported directly to General Henry H. Arnold, commanding general of Army Air Forces. Initially this aerial campaign was staged from India through air bases constructed by Army engineers in central China. In mid-1944, the campaign shifted to the Mariana Islands. The United States also supported two adjacent Allied theaters: China and Southeast Asia. These multiple campaigns, which reflected divergent strategic goals, could only have been possible by the capability of the United States to sustain more than one simultaneous drive.

In the North Pacific, the United States had to defend Alaska and the Aleutian Islands. But in order to take on that mission, the Army Corps of Engineers had to first build a land route to Alaska. The Army organized an engineer brigade with seven engineer regiments for the unprecedented construction project. In just seven months, they carved out over fifteen hundred miles of road through peat bogs and permafrost, through forests and mountains, and over untamed rivers. The first convoy traveled the completed road in November 1942. In May 1943, the 7th Infantry Division, which had trained for amphibious operations at Fort Ord, California, recaptured Attu at a cost of 550 killed in action and 1,150 wounded. In August, a larger force of American and Canadian soldiers, including the U.S.-Canadian First Special Service Force, landed on Kiska, but found the Japanese defenders had already left. Soon after, the Joint Chiefs of Staff dropped plans for a separate northern thrust against Japan, and Alaska lost priority.

On the Asian mainland, World War II had begun in July 1937, when Japan invaded China and quickly captured coastal areas and major cities. The Chinese Nationalist and Communist forces agreed to an uneasy cease-fire to confront the invaders. The United States began economic and military aid and established a military mission. At first, the United States sent lend-lease supplies through Rangoon (Yangon), until the Japanese captured Burma (Myanmar), leaving only the air route, flying "the Hump" over the Himalaya Mountains.

Logistics remained a key constraint on operations in this landlocked theater, and much of the tonnage was dedicated to the air campaign. While airmen conducted the largest airlift up to that time, fifteen thousand American soldiers built a highway through rugged mountains from northeast India to southwestern China. The first convoy over the Ledo Road arrived in Kunming on 4 February 1945.

Stilwell served as chief of staff to the Chinese president; commander of U.S. forces in China, Burma, and India; and commander of Chinese and American combat forces in Burma. He had served three previous tours in China, spoke Mandarin, and had served as Army attaché to Peking during the 1937 Japanese invasion. Even so, he found his new assignment challenging, with complex command arrangements and the sensitivities of advising the Chinese government. Stilwell sought to train and equip the Chinese Nationalist Army. At Ramgarh in northeast India, American advisers trained two Chinese divisions that were committed into combat in northern Burma. The Army even sent a small liaison and observer mission to the Chinese Communist headquarters in Yenan (Yan'an).

In India, the Army created a vast logistical and training base, including port facilities, rail lines, airfields, pipelines, and depots, in support of operations in China and Burma. Those serving in the Office of Strategic Services Detachment 101 were among the first Americans to see combat in Southeast Asia. Composed of Americans and Kachin tribesmen from the Burma hill country, they began operations behind Japanese lines early in 1943. In February 1944, the Allies established the Northern Combat Area Command for American, British, and Chinese forces in northern Burma. The United States agreed to commit a regimental-sized American unit, the 5307th Composite Unit (Provisional). Dubbed by American reporters "Merrill's Marauders" after its commander, Brig. Gen. Frank D. Merrill, the unit, together with two Chinese divisions, in February 1944 penetrated deep behind Japanese lines. In May, they captured the Japanese airfield at Myitkyina, which was threatening the airlift to China. In the ensuing battle, the unit suffered terrible losses with few reinforcements. The Northern Combat Area Command later committed two additional American regiments, but not until Merrill's Marauders had been rendered combat ineffective.

Allied hopes for the China Theater failed to materialize and led to distrust and mutual recriminations. In April 1944, a powerful

Japanese offensive shattered the Chinese Army and overran several American-built air bases. In June 1944, the Twentieth Air Force began sending B–29s from India and China against strategic targets in Japan and elsewhere in the region, but by the end of the year, the strategic bombardment campaign shifted to the Mariana Islands, which were less vulnerable and more logistically sustainable. In October 1944, after months of friction, the Chinese government requested Stilwell's replacement. He was replaced by Lt. Gen. Albert C. Wedemeyer, who also commanded U.S. Forces, China. Stilwell's deputy, Lt. Gen. Daniel I. Sultan, took command of U.S. Forces, India-Burma.

Wedemeyer planned a new Chinese offensive for early 1945 and established the Chinese Combat Command, with adviser teams down to the division level, totaling about thirty-one hundred soldiers and airmen. Each team had twenty-five officers and fifty enlisted men, including an air-ground liaison team with dedicated communications for air support. He also established a Chinese Training Command. That spring, an American-trained-and-equipped Chinese force turned back a Japanese offensive and began a push toward the coast. By August 1945, the Army had about sixty thousand air and ground soldiers stationed in China.

As American capabilities expanded in the Pacific, the Army conducted larger, more complex joint operations at even greater distances than before, using corps and army headquarters for command and control, while repositioning its lines of communications. After Guadalcanal, operations continued in the South Pacific for another year. In November 1943, the 3d Marine Division landed on Bougainville, then handed off the island to the Army's XIV Corps. By the time the Japanese defenders counterattacked in March 1944, the XIV Corps had two divisions well dug-in and backed by eight artillery battalions and sixteen additional batteries. American firepower completely destroyed the attackers. Japanese losses amounted to over 5,000 killed, compared to 263 American soldiers killed. After this victory, the United States reassigned the American forces to other theaters and turned over subsequent operations in the Solomon Islands to the 3d New Zealand Division.

In the Central Pacific, the offensive phase began on November 1943 with an attack on the Gilbert Islands, the first major opposed landings in the Navy's "island-hopping" strategy. The 2d Marine Division deployed from New Zealand to attack Tarawa, while the

27th Infantry Division deployed from Hawaii to attack Makin Atoll. Both assault forces used the new amphibious tractors, popularly called alligators, to cross the coral reef. The 27th Infantry Division was accompanied by the Army's first field historian, Lt. Col. S. L. A. Marshall, to collect combat lessons from the battlefield.

The Central Pacific offensive continued on 1 February 1944 with attacks in the Marshall Islands. The 4th Marine Division attacked Roi and Namur Islands, while the 7th Infantry Division, reconstituted after the Aleutians, attacked Kwajalein. In June and July 1944, Admiral Nimitz attacked his biggest targets yet on Japan's inner line of defense in the Mariana Islands: Saipan, Tinian, and Guam. The battle on Saipan was marred by interservice rivalry, when the corps commander, Marine Lt. Gen. Holland M. "Howling Mad" Smith, relieved the commander of the 27th Infantry Division, Army Maj. Gen. Ralph C. Smith, citing his division's poor performance. The battle was won after three weeks of bitter fighting, but Army officers remained outraged by the general's relief. An Army investigation concluded that the relief was "not justified by the facts," and transferred General Smith out of the theater. The controversy "produced a crisis in interservice relations that poisoned Marine Corps–Army relations for the rest of the war," according to historian Allan R. Millett, "and even fueled postwar interservice controversies."

The battle for Saipan was unusual for another reason as well. For the first time in the Pacific fighting, soldiers and marines encountered civilians in significant numbers. Thousands were killed in the fighting and thousands of Japanese civilians killed themselves rather than surrender to American soldiers and marines. The Americans captured about seventeen hundred prisoners of war, many of whom turned out to be civilians, not Japanese soldiers.

Saipan, Tinian, and Guam became the hub of American naval and air power in the Central Pacific. The U.S. Pacific Fleet moved to Guam, and Nimitz moved his advanced headquarters from Pearl Harbor to Guam as well. Army engineers scraped out air bases that enabled B–29 bombers to strike the Japanese home islands, the first raid being launched in November. Army and Navy engineers and medical personnel created a hospital network with nine thousand beds for the costly campaigns to come.

Halfway between the Mariana Islands and Tokyo lay the volcanic island of Iwo Jima. On 19 February 1945, three marine divisions assaulted the island. They destroyed the Japanese garrison of twenty-one thousand and captured the island's airfields with help from Army support units, including three African American amphibious truck companies, nineteen of whose soldiers were awarded the Silver Star.

In the Southwest Pacific in April 1944, MacArthur's forces, guided by signals intelligence and supported by the Fifth Air Force and Seventh Fleet, leapfrogged four hundred miles along the north coast of New Guinea to land two divisions near Hollandia and cut off the *Japanese Eighteenth Army*. In July and August, the Japanese counterattacked fiercely along the Driniumor River. The Americans suffered heavy casualties; four soldiers were awarded the Medal of Honor. The Japanese attackers were destroyed with nearly ten thousand killed and thousands more left to starve in the jungle.

Other American forces conducted regimental- and division-sized landings in the Bismarck Archipelago and Admiralty Islands northeast of New Guinea. On 27 May 1944, the 41st Infantry Division attacked Biak Island farther west to gain its three airfields, but the Japanese fought hard from well-prepared positions in deep caves. Almost three weeks later, the division had still failed to dislodge the defenders. The Sixth Army commander, Lt. Gen. Walter Krueger, sent Eichelberger, the I Corps commander, to take personal command as he had at Buna. Eichelberger flew to Biak and ordered the corps staff to follow at once. "Moving a corps headquarters on fire-alarm notice is no easy job," Eichelberger wrote, but the corps staff followed by boat the next day. He took charge, assessed the situation, relieved the division commander, and reorganized the attack. By the time the island was secured, the Americans had killed all forty-eight hundred Japanese defenders. The Army learned to use coordinated amphibious and airborne operations to keep up relentless pressure. To capture more airfields, in July 1944, the 158th Regimental Combat Team assaulted Noemfoor Island from the sea, while the 503d Parachute Infantry landed from the air. Together, they killed 1,759 Japanese and captured another 889.

In two years, MacArthur's forces had advanced half the distance back to the Philippines. Army logisticians shifted their base of supply from Australia to Hollandia, where Army engineers constructed vast facilities where nothing had existed before. The Army left Australia and New Zealand almost as rapidly as it had come. Army headquarters and support units had come to rely on

Australian women for administrative and clerical jobs, but their government would not allow them to deploy to forward areas. To solve this dilemma, the Southwest Pacific Area requested Women's Army Corps soldiers from the United States. The first group arrived in May 1944 and their number eventually grew to fifty-five hundred.

MANY D-DAYS IN THE PACIFIC, 1944–1945

In October 1944, the Sixth Army attacked Leyte in the Philippines with two corps and six divisions, putting more men ashore on the first day than the Allies had in Normandy four months earlier. For this, the largest ground campaign to date in the Pacific, American forces crossed hundreds of miles of open ocean to reach the landing beaches. MacArthur made good on his

Soldiers unload supplies on Leyte in the Philippines, 21 October 1944.

promise to the people of the Philippines. Initially, the Americans were unable to establish air and maritime superiority, so the Japanese were able to bring reinforcements from elsewhere in the Philippines and as far away as Japan and China. Fierce fighting continued for ten weeks before the island was declared secure.

In January 1945, the Sixth Army invaded Luzon with two corps and a force that eventually counted eleven divisions. In four weeks, forward units reached Manila, which the Japanese decided to defend. For nearly a month, the 1st Cavalry Division, 37th Infantry Division, and 11th Airborne Division fought house-to-house to destroy the Japanese defenders, resulting in the total destruction of the city of eight hundred thousand and its old walled inner city, Intramuros, which the Americans had captured in 1898. Near the end of the battle, MacArthur announced the reestablishment of the Commonwealth of the Philippines. "Your capital city," he told a provisional assembly of prominent Filipinos, "cruelly punished though it be, has regained its rightful place—citadel of democracy in the East."

The campaign for Luzon continued to the end of the war. Soldiers fought a sustained campaign to defeat Japanese forces on the large island. Philippine guerrillas provided vital intelligence and combat power. The largest group, called U.S. Army Forces in the Philippines (North Luzon), numbered up to eighteen thousand irregulars and was led by Col. Russell W. Volckmann. Volckmann, a graduate of the U.S. Military Academy, had refused to surrender in 1942 and stayed behind to organize resistance. In southern Luzon, the 11th Airborne Division conducted several combat jumps, and in February 1945, the 503d Parachute Regimental Combat Team seized the fortress of Corregidor, which had surrendered to the Japanese three years before.

While the Sixth Army conquered Luzon, the Eighth Army conducted more than fifty amphibious assaults to recapture the southern Philippines. The largest came in April, when the X Corps attacked Mindanao, the large southern island where the Japanese had expected the first American attack. The 24th and 31st Infantry Divisions were aided by a guerrilla force of twenty-four thousand, led by an Army Reserve engineer officer, Lt. Col. Wendell W. Fertig, who had refused to surrender in 1942.

In this way, the Army returned to the country it had pacified and garrisoned for decades. The towns and countryside had suffered terrible destruction from the fighting of 1941–1942, the harsh years of Japanese occupation and guerrilla war, and the liberation in 1944–1945. The Sixth Army used thirteen Philippine civil affairs units, staffed in part by exiled Filipinos recruited in the United States, for humanitarian assistance.

For the next campaign, the War Department activated the Tenth Army in Hawaii. On Easter Sunday, 1 April 1945, Lt. Gen. Simon Bolivar Buckner Jr. landed the Army's XXIV Corps and the III Marine Amphibious Corps on Okinawa, for a total of 183,000 troops. Soldiers and marines fought three months of intense combat that came to resemble the trench fighting and heavy artillery barrages on the western front during World War I. The Japanese defenders could not hope to defeat the Americans but were determined to demonstrate that any invasion of the Japanese home islands would be unthinkable. Perhaps as many as 110,000 Japanese combatants died in the fighting, as did an estimated 42,000 civilians. The Japanese inflicted 49,151 casualties on the attackers, including 12,520 killed or missing. On 18 June, Buckner himself was mortally wounded when a Japanese shell hit near a forward observation post he was visiting. Marine Lt. Gen. Roy S. Geiger assumed temporary command of the Tenth Army for five days until the arrival of General Stilwell, returning to the Pacific eight months after leaving China.

Luzon and Okinawa became launch pads for the planned invasion of Japan. On 3 April 1945, the Joint Chiefs of Staff designated MacArthur as the Commander in Chief, Army Forces in the Pacific, and he began planning for Operation OLYMPIC, the invasion of the southernmost island, Kyushu, scheduled for 1 November. When Germany surrendered in May, the War Department prepared to redeploy fifteen divisions and their supporting forces to the Pacific.

IN THE RUINS OF EMPIRE, 1945–1949

On 6 August 1945, the Twentieth Air Force sent a B–29 from the Mariana Islands to drop an atomic bomb over Hiroshima. The bomb destroyed the port city and immediately killed between 70,000 and 80,000 people. Three days later, another bomb was dropped over Nagasaki, destroying the city and killing more than 35,000 people. In both cities, tens of thousands more died over the coming months of acute radiation exposure and other injuries.

These two bombs, products of America's scientific, industrial, and organizational prowess, changed the face of Asia. On 9 August, the Soviet Union declared war on Japan and the Red Army attacked Manchuria, destroying in weeks the Japanese dream of an empire on the continent of Asia. Japan gave its unconditional surrender on 14 August.

On 30 August, the 11th Airborne Division airlifted to Atsugi naval air station near Tokyo, while the Third Fleet landed the 4th Marines at Yokosuka naval base. MacArthur accepted the Japanese surrender on 2 September. Harried staff officers quickly rewrote the movement plans for Operation OLYMPIC for unopposed landings, sometimes across the same beaches they had been planning to attack. Combat and combat support forces earmarked for the invasion of Japan were rushed to Japan, Korea, and China. While policymakers in Washington considered new policies for the postwar world, soldiers on the ground dealt with local issues as they arose.

Local Army commanders accepted the surrender of Japanese forces throughout the region in dozens of local surrender ceremonies. The Office of Strategic Services flew small teams throughout the region to liberate prisoner-of-war camps, while the Army repatriated about thirty-six thousand Allied military personnel and civilian internees. The Army supervised the demobilization of 7 million Japanese soldiers and sailors, half of whom were still overseas, and repatriated 1.2 million foreign workers in Japan and its empire. The Counter Intelligence Corps eliminated the feared Japanese military police and gathered evidence for war crimes trials that were conducted by Army judge advocates in Manila, Tokyo, and Yokohama.

While managing these postconflict responsibilities of bewildering complexity, the Army dismantled itself. On 1 September 1945, Army ground and air forces in the region included 1,460,000 soldiers in the Pacific; 196,000 in India-Burma and China; and 38,000 in Alaska. Soldiers and their congressmen clamored for their rapid demobilization and return. In January 1946, the War Department announced a slowdown of redeployments, causing soldier morale to plummet. On 6 January 1946, twenty thousand American soldiers held a mass demonstration in Manila to protest the slowdown, as did others on Guam, in Hawaii, and elsewhere in the region. Selective Service continued to draft young men who now were urgently needed to replace returning veterans.

41

While the Army was absorbed in these tasks, the region was plunged into turmoil. British, French, and Dutch armies returned to reclaim their colonial possessions, but their empires never recovered from the impact of war and occupation. The Japanese "Greater East Asia Co-prosperity Sphere" vanished as quickly as it had arrived. The former colonial powers, themselves devastated by the war, needed their former colonies and worried about rising nationalism and communist subversion. The old order had collapsed, but the new order was not yet visible. When the United Nations was founded in 1945, only five independent countries joined from the region: China was given a permanent seat on the Security Council, but the country soon slid back into civil war; Australia, India, New Zealand, and the Philippines were still moving toward full sovereignty. Three more joined by 1950 and six more by 1960 as the region shifted slowly and painfully from an arena of colonial rivalries to a zone of independent states.

The focus of U.S. national security planning adapted to the profoundly altered strategic landscape. Japan, no longer a threat, had to be occupied. Its industrial power had to be restored and preserved from absorption into the Soviet sphere of influence. The Soviet Union, which had conquered Manchuria with eighty divisions, threatened to upset American plans. China was embroiled in civil war. A permanent American presence in the region seemed vital to national security.

At the same time, the Army had its own institutional concerns. "World War II proved to be the army's finest hour," writes historian Brian McAllister Linn. "Yet at this moment of greatest triumph, the explosion of the atomic bomb at Hiroshima dramatically redefined modern warfare, making the army and 'conventional warfare' seem irrelevant." The Army had helped defeat Japan as part of a joint team. Yet in the final analysis, it was not clear how much the Army had contributed to victory. In the public eye, it was the marines who had captured Guadalcanal, Iwo Jima, and Okinawa. The Navy could point to the destruction of Japan's navy and merchant marine. The Air Force, which became an independent service in 1947, could point to the destruction of Japan's cities from the air and to a terrifying new weapon. Navy and Air Force leaders convinced themselves that Japan had been on the verge of surrender with no need for a costly invasion. The Army suddenly did seem almost irrelevant.

The Army's most pressing task was to occupy Japan and enforce the surrender terms, something the Navy and Air Force could not do. Over seventy million Japanese were exhausted by eight years of war, by the destruction of their cities and merchant fleet, by the stripping away of their overseas empire and traditional economic relations, and by the utter discrediting of their rulers. On 14 August 1945, the Joint Chiefs of Staff designated MacArthur as Supreme Commander for the Allied Powers (SCAP). He rushed thirteen Army and two Marine Corps divisions to Japan. He gave the honor of marching into Tokyo to the 1st Cavalry Division. It soon became clear that the occupation forces would face no armed resistance. Within months, Army units and headquarters were hollowed out by rapid demobilization. By the end of 1945, some 286,000 American soldiers remained in Japan. The Sixth Army was inactivated in January 1946, leaving the Eighth Army to conduct the occupation. In January 1946, the Eighth Army lost 48,830 soldiers and received only 1,385 replacements. By 1948, the Army's occupation strength dropped to 91,000. Most Marine Corps units left Japan by the spring of 1946. The British agreed to send occupation forces, which began to arrive in February 1946. The British Commonwealth Occupation Force assigned to southern Japan included brigades from Britain, Australia, New Zealand, and India. The Soviet Union asked for the northern island of Hokkaido as an occupation zone, but the United States refused to give them any share in the occupation.

MacArthur's General Headquarters (GHQ) undertook America's largest nation-building project since the Philippines. A small team of Army Reserve officers and civilians under Army Reserve Col. Charles L. Kades in the GHQ Government Section wrote a new constitution for Japan in February 1946. GHQ supervised a general election in April 1946. Within two years, occupation officials began to talk of a "reverse course," as Japan was miraculously transformed from a defeated enemy to a valuable ally. Some even talked of a peace treaty and an end to the occupation. For the Eighth Army, occupation duty became easier. The Army assigned several thousand Japanese American soldiers who used their language and cultural skills to bridge the two cultures. In late 1946, the War Department allowed officers and noncommissioned officers to bring their families to Japan, where they lived in requisitioned housing and enjoyed inexpensive domestic staff. "Life in the 'colonial army' took on traditional form," wrote historian Roy K. Flint. With the arrival of families, "the social routine that developed was similar in every way to patterns in the Philippines and China before World War II. Virtually overnight, the Occupation Army became a nine-to-five organization." The occupation also had a dark underside of black market, drug abuse, and crimes against civilians. But in general, the occupation was widely perceived to be a success, in large part due to the Army.

While the Army ran the occupation, policymakers in Washington focused on the emerging Cold War in Europe. Between May 1946 and October 1949, no member of the Joint Chiefs of Staff visited Tokyo; nor did MacArthur return to the United States until 1951. MacArthur, like his counterpart in Germany, General Lucius D. Clay, "occupied, in reality, highly independent positions," wrote George F. Kennan, chief of the State Department Planning Staff. "They would not have admitted it, but they were virtually laws unto themselves."

The United States separated Okinawa from Japan, but the destruction of battle would take many years to repair. The surviving population of over three hundred thousand lived mostly in refugee camps. American military strength on Okinawa peaked in August 1945 at 259,000. One year later, the number had declined to 20,000, and by August 1949 to 12,500. The Navy handed over administration of the islands to the Army on 1 July 1946. Nature itself added to Okinawa's sufferings: fierce typhoons struck the island in 1948 and again in 1949, causing extensive damage. It seemed as if Okinawa might never recover. In 1949, the Army activated the 29th Regimental Combat Team on Okinawa.

The former Japanese colony of Korea posed different challenges. The United States and Soviet Union agreed to a temporary dividing line along the 38th Parallel, with the Soviets disarming Japanese forces north of the line and American forces to the south. In September 1945, the Tenth Army deployed the XXIV Corps from Okinawa to set up the U.S. Army Military Government in Korea, which established the Korean Constabulary in January 1946. When the Republic of Korea was established in the south on 15 August 1948, the United States terminated the military government. In the north, the Democratic People's Republic of Korea was established. But deep-rooted problems remained. In the south, a civil war erupted and both regimes indulged in cross-border raids. But neither the United States nor the Soviet Union desired to be drawn into local quarrels and withdrew by 1949.

Seoul Street Scene, *by Steven R. Kidd, 1945, depicting two soldiers with the* U.S. occupation forces

In August 1948, the Army had established a provisional military advisory group to help create a new South Korean army. On 1 July 1949, the provisional group became the Korea Military Advisory Group with about five hundred officers and noncommissioned officers. By June 1950, they had begun to train eight light infantry divisions. In June 1949, the Joint Chiefs of Staff called for a regional defense based on an "offshore island chain," and on 16 February 1950, the Joint Chiefs removed Korea from MacArthur's area of responsibility.

In the Philippines, the United States kept its promise to grant independence. During the last months of the war, the Army reconstituted the Philippine Army and Philippine Scouts under U.S. command. But as the Philippines gained independence on 4 July 1946, the War Department separated the Philippine Army from the U.S. Army and demobilized its soldiers, many of whom had served under U.S. command in 1941–1942 and again in 1944–1946. The Philippine Scouts, a statutory component of the U.S. Army, reorganized some units in the fall of 1945 and added others. By October 1946, over twenty thousand Filipinos had enlisted in the Scouts. For the first time, the Army deployed Scout units elsewhere in the region, including one thousand in the Marianas and five thousand in the Ryukyus. However, in 1947 the War Department halted further enlistments. In 1949, it offered seven hundred enlisted

45

Scouts transfers to the Regular Army and discharged the others. The last Philippine Scout units were inactivated in the early 1950s.

The new Philippine government looked critically at retaining U.S. bases. After hard bargaining, in March 1947 the Philippines and the United States signed an agreement that allowed the Air Force to retain Clark Field and the Navy to retain Subic Bay. The Army asked to retain Fort William McKinley, but the Philippine government refused. Instead, on a portion of the renamed Fort Bonifacio the American Battle Monuments Commission built the American Cemetery and Memorial, America's only overseas military cemetery in the region. The Army headquarters was replaced by a joint U.S. military advisory group.

China, for many years the focus of America's hopes and dreams in Asia, was an area of great uncertainty as the war ended. The Joint Chiefs of Staff sent fifty thousand marines from the III Marine Amphibious Corps to stabilize North China. The Army Air Forces and Navy transported more than four hundred thousand Nationalist troops to north China and the coastal areas to seize areas under Japanese control and block Communist troops. The conflict between the Nationalists and Communists threatened to flare up again, and the United States feared becoming involved. On 25 August 1945, Communist soldiers killed U.S. Army Capt. John Birch, a former Baptist missionary serving with the Office of Strategic Services. His death, little noted at the time, was later remembered as the first casualty of the Cold War in Asia by the anti-Communist John Birch Society.

In December 1945, President Harry S. Truman sent General Marshall to China to mediate, and he worked for a year to bring both sides to a compromise. In early 1946, Truman authorized a U.S. Army advisory group, but that summer, to put pressure on America's wartime ally, the United States halted arms shipments. Even Marshall's talents were not sufficient to reach a peaceful resolution. The civil war resumed in April 1946, and Nationalist forces initially gained the upper hand, but during 1947, they suffered severe reverses. The Nationalists consolidated their hold on Taiwan, where the U.S. Army advisory group established a ground forces training center in December 1947. By late 1948, the situation was lost. "Military matériel and economic aid," wrote Maj. Gen. David G. Barr, the group chief, "in my opinion is less important to the salvation of China than other factors. No battle has been lost since my arrival due to lack of ammunition or equipment." In 1949, the Chinese Communists drove the Nationalists off the mainland and established the People's Republic of China. The United States became embroiled in a bitter controversy over "who lost China," that poisoned domestic politics for years.

Elsewhere in the region, the Army reestablished itself to meet the new realities. Hawaii remained the keystone to regional defense. The Army reorganized the Hawaii Army National Guard in 1946 and activated the 5th Regimental Combat Team at Schofield Barracks in 1949. When the war ended, construction was already under way on the 1,500-bed Tripler General Hospital. When the hospital was completed in 1948, it became the centerpiece of the Army medical system in the region. The Corps of Engineers also built the National Memorial Cemetery of the Pacific in the Punchbowl overlooking Honolulu, which in 1949 became the final resting place for thousands of servicemen who had died in the Pacific.

Military strength in Alaska declined from a wartime high of about 150,000 to 13,000 in 1946. However, the military left behind new infrastructure, including a modernized rail system, roads, and airfields. In 1949, the Army stationed the 4th Regimental Combat Team at Fort Richardson and reorganized the Alaska National Guard, including the specialized Arctic experience of the Eskimo Scouts in the 207th Infantry Group.

Postwar defense planning took place in a rapidly changing bureaucratic environment. In late 1946, the Joint Chiefs of Staff established three unified commands: Far East Command (FECOM) in Tokyo; Pacific Command (PACOM) at Camp H. M. Smith, Hawaii; and Alaskan Command (ALCOM) at Elmendorf Air Force Base, Alaska. On 1 January 1947, FECOM was given responsibility for all U.S. forces in Japan, Korea, the Ryukyus, the Philippines, the Marianas, and the Bonins. The Air Force became independent in September 1947, which required Army forces in the Pacific to divide into separate Army and Air Force elements, from logistics to engineers to intelligence. At the same time, the renamed Department of the Army was incorporated into a new National Military Establishment, soon renamed the Department of Defense.

By 1949, the Army's posture in the Far East was significantly different from what it had been before 1941. Japan was the new center of America's security framework in Northeast Asia. China had fallen to the Communists. The United States retained Okinawa and Guam. The Philippines allowed American air and naval bases, but no Army bases. Hawaii remained the anchor. The Army now had four understrength divisions in Japan, one regimental combat team on Okinawa, one in Hawaii, and another in Alaska. In Japan, the new Eighth Army commander, Lt. Gen. Walton H. Walker, began a rigorous training program to prepare his units to defend against a possible Soviet invasion.

America's national leaders came to believe the country's security rested on its atomic monopoly and began using remote South Pacific islands to test the next generation of atomic weapons. The Army supported Operation CROSSROADS, which conducted atomic tests at Bikini Atoll beginning in July 1946.

But America's atomic monopoly could not last. In September 1949, an Air Force reconnaissance aircraft flying from Misawa, Japan, to Eilson Air Force Base, Alaska, detected traces of a Soviet atomic test in distant Central Asia. Years ahead of expectations, the Soviet Union had become the world's second atomic power. The balance of power in Asia would soon shift once again.

Journalist Frank Gibney later wrote: "If the map of East Asia seemed to have stabilized by 1949, this was an illusion. Life within the new countries continued to be in turmoil. Two major international wars were on the way, not to mention a rash of revolts, confrontations, and border skirmishes. . . . Ironically, it was Japan, the country that had thrown the Asia-Pacific world into chaos, that now began to seem an island of stability."

HOT AND COLD WARS, 1950–1973

KOREAN WAR, 1950–1953

On 25 June 1950, Korean Communist leader Kim Il Sung launched the *North Korean People's Army* across the 38th Parallel to unify his country by force. The civil war that had simmered since 1948 burst into flames with global repercussions. The Communists had the advantage of T34 tanks from their Soviet allies and tens of thousands of veteran Korean soldiers who until recently had fought in the Chinese civil war. Once again, the United States was caught by surprise. General MacArthur urgently requested help, and President Truman quickly authorized a military response, telling an aide: "There's no telling what they'll do, if we don't put up a fight right now." With this decision, Truman extended the Cold War policy of containment from Europe to Asia. *(Map 3)*

In the opening days, the inexperienced and poorly equipped South Korean Army crumpled and U.S. air attacks from Japan failed to stem the tide. Seoul fell on the fourth day. The United Nations Security Council asked its members to "furnish such assistance to the Republic of Korea as may be necessary to repel the armed attack and to restore international peace and security in the area." Korea was where the Cold War first became hot.

The Eighth Army threw its units into the maelstrom as fast as they could move from their garrisons in sleepy Japanese towns. First into the fight was the 1st Battalion, 21st Infantry, of the 24th

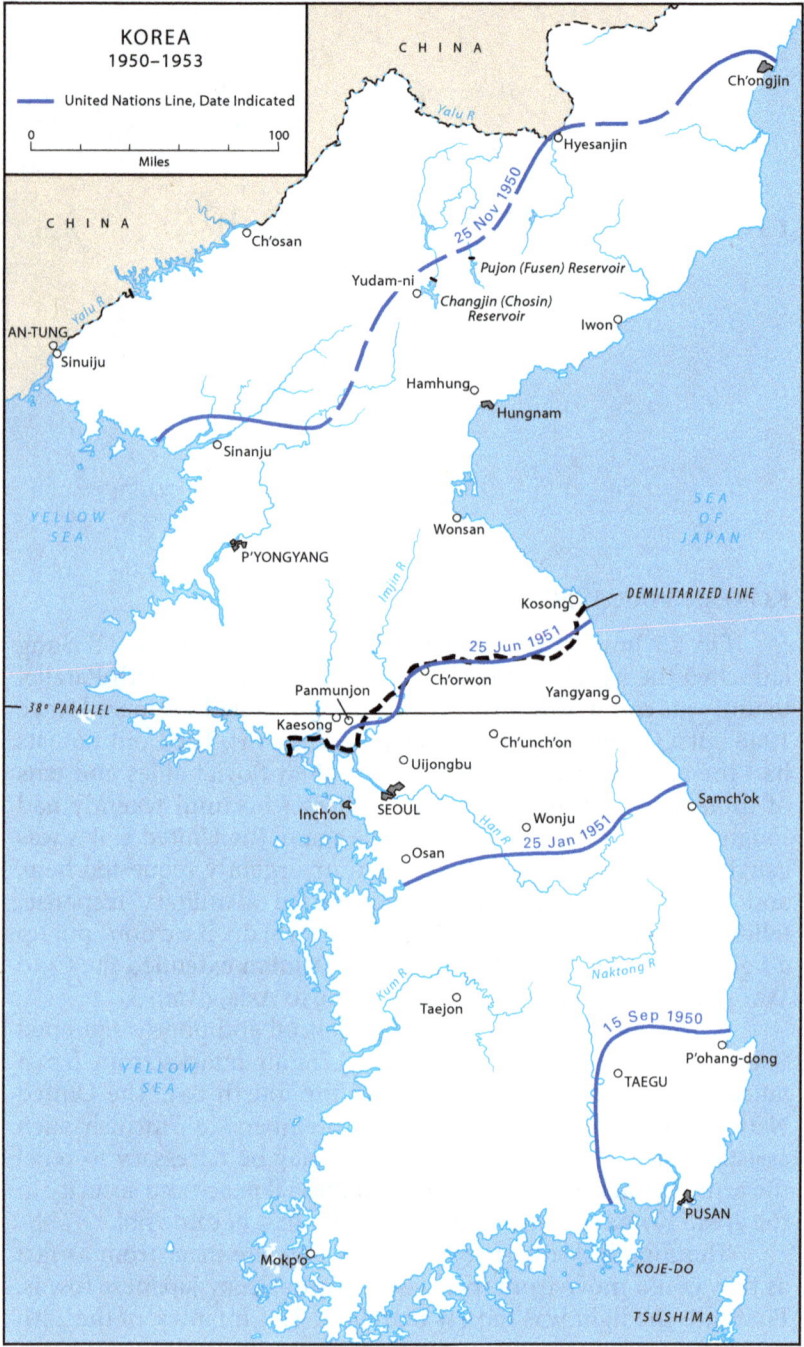

KOREA
1950–1953

United Nations Line, Date Indicated

0 ———————— 100
Miles

CHINA

Yalu R.

Ch'ongjin

Hyesanjin

25 Nov 1950

Ch'osan

Pujon (Fusen) Reservoir

Yudam-ni

Changjin (Chosin) Reservoir

Iwon

AN-TUNG

Sinuiju

Hamhung

Hungnam

Sinanju

YELLOW SEA

Wonsan

SEA OF JAPAN

P'YONGYANG

Imjin R.

Kosong

DEMILITARIZED LINE

25 Jun 1951

Panmunjon

Ch'orwon

Yangyang

38° PARALLEL

Kaesong

Ch'unch'on

Uijongbu

Inch'on

SEOUL

Wonju

Samch'ok

25 Jan 1951

Osan

Han R.

Kum R.

Naktong R.

Taejon

15 Sep 1950

P'ohang-dong

YELLOW SEA

TAEGU

PUSAN

Mokp'o

KOJE-DO

TSUSHIMA

Map 3

Infantry Division, commanded by Lt. Col. Charles B. Smith. Task Force SMITH set up a blocking position north of Osan on 5 July with two rifle companies and a battery of 105-mm. howitzers, only to watch helplessly as enemy tanks rolled through their position and enemy infantry outflanked them. Outnumbered and inadequately equipped, the 540-man task force suffered over 180 casualties and lost all its vehicles and equipment other than small arms. The remainder of the division was severely mauled, losing 1,150 men as it fought a covering force action for sixty miles during two weeks of hard fighting. Some American units disintegrated as their soldiers "bugged out," rather than stand and fight. Leaders struggled to maintain control. While evacuating Taejon, the division commander, Maj. Gen. William F. Dean, became separated from his command and evaded capture for thirty-six days before being taken prisoner.

The Eighth Army fought back to a perimeter around the southern port of Pusan (Busan), joined by the 1st Provisional Marine Brigade from Camp Pendleton, California, and surviving elements of the Republic of Korea Army. Lt. Gen. Walton H. Walker directed the defense of the perimeter, while the valiant efforts of the American and South Korean defenders under scorching summer skies bought precious time to deploy additional American forces from Japan, as well as the 5th Regimental Combat Team from Hawaii, two battalions of the 29th Regimental Combat Team from Okinawa, and the 2d Infantry Division from Fort Lewis, Washington. Meanwhile, the president reinstituted draft calls and called up much of the Army Reserve and four National Guard divisions plus many nondivisional units. Many of these citizen-soldiers augmented Army forces in the continental United States or Europe. Army logisticians began to build up the theater support system, including port and rail operations and an equipment rebuild program in Japan. The United States built an international coalition that grew to more than twenty countries. In addition to air, naval, and medical forces, more than a dozen countries sent ground combat troops; Britain, Canada, and Turkey committed full brigades.

During the war against Japan, MacArthur had learned the value of bold amphibious maneuver. On 26 August, he activated the X Corps for just such a counterstroke. On 15 September, the X Corps launched Operation CHROMITE, landing at Inch'on (Incheon) with the 7th Infantry Division, augmented with 8,652

Unloading supplies and equipment at Inch'on, Korea, September 1950

South Korean draftees, and the 1st Marine Division with one South Korean marine regiment. The Eighth Army attacked from the south and the North Korean forces reeled back. Within weeks, the United Nations forces liberated Seoul, then drove north of the 38th Parallel to the Chinese border on the Yalu River. On 25–29 October, the X Corps conducted another landing, this time in the northeast near Wonsan. By November, the Eighth Army was poised to drive the Communist regime into exile and complete the unification of the country.

The unexpected United Nations advance alarmed both China and the Soviet Union and triggered a decisive intervention by those powers. Mao Tse-tung (Mao Zedong) sent a massive Chinese ground force into the fight and Stalin sent the Soviet Air Force to provide air cover. The Chinese attacked the Eighth Army on the night of 25 November. In the chaos of battle, the Republic of Korea's II Corps collapsed in the center of the United Nations line. The 2d U.S. Infantry Division narrowly escaped total destruction, losing one-third of its men killed, wounded, or missing and most of its equipment. In the northeast, the 1st Marine Division and one regimental combat team of the 7th Infantry Division fought

Soldiers of Company F, 9th Infantry, 2d Infantry Division, climb "Bloody Ridge," summer 1951.

out of entrapment around the Chosin (Changjin) Reservoir at a heavy cost. The Eighth Army withdrew to positions just north of Seoul. On 23 December, while visiting forward units, General Walker was killed when a South Korean truck struck his jeep.

On 26 December, Lt. Gen. Matthew B. Ridgway took command of the Eighth Army. As long supply lines and relentless air attacks stalled the Chinese offensive, General Ridgway revitalized his demoralized command. He insisted on an aggressive spirit and the maximum use of firepower and relieved commanders who had become exhausted or ineffective. In January 1951, he began a cautious counterattack using "meat grinder" tactics to inflict maximum casualties.

Author T. R. Fehrenbach later summed up the paradox of the Korean War in the nuclear age: "Americans in 1950 rediscovered something that since Hiroshima they had forgotten: You may fly over a land forever; you may bomb it, atomize it, pulverize it and wipe it clean of life—but if you desire to defend it, protect it, and keep it for civilization, you must do this on the ground, the way the Roman legions did, by putting your young men into the mud."

As America's young men fought in the mud and snow, President Truman and his advisers were determined not to allow the war to become World War III. This limited kind of war perplexed soldiers and the public alike and led to an unprecedented crisis in civil-military relations. Truman declined to ask Congress for a declaration of war, but instead called the intervention a "police action" by the international community to enforce collective security. Truman dispatched the Seventh Fleet to prevent the Chinese Communists from attacking Taiwan, but

53

declined Chiang Kai-shek's offer of Nationalist troops for South Korea. The Joint Chiefs of Staff rejected MacArthur's requests to bomb enemy airfields in Manchuria. An all-out war with China, Chairman of the Joint Chiefs of Staff General Omar N. Bradley later told Congress, "would involve us in the wrong war, at the wrong place, at the wrong time, and with the wrong enemy." While sending reinforcements to the Far East, Truman simultaneously built up forces in Europe, activating the Seventh Army in Germany. In March 1951, as United Nations forces liberated Seoul and approached the 38th Parallel, Truman pursued a cease-fire. MacArthur disagreed vehemently with these political restrictions and his opinions soon become public. "If we lose this war to Communism in Asia the fall of Europe is inevitable," he wrote to a congressman. "There is no substitute for victory." Truman viewed the world situation very differently and dismissed the 71-year-old theater commander, who had become the symbol of America's past achievements in the Far East.

In April and May 1951, the Chinese launched major offensives, but this time the United Nations Command was ready with a powerful counterattack. Now, along with its allies, the United States had six Army divisions and one marine division backed by extensive artillery and air support. Ridgway followed MacArthur at FECOM, and Lt. Gen. James A. Van Fleet took over the Eighth Army after having led U.S. military assistance to Greece during its civil war. The United Nations Command defeated the Chinese offensives and in June stabilized the front near the 38th Parallel. Armistice talks began in July at the village of Panmunjom, but the fighting continued for two more years, as each side sought to gain ground to influence the negotiations.

This was a new kind of war in many ways. It was the first war conducted under the 1947 reorganization that had created the Department of Defense and Central Intelligence Agency, formalized the Joint Chiefs of Staff, and created an independent Air Force. Wartime pressures to keep units manned compelled the Army to implement Truman's 1948 executive order ending segregation. By the armistice, the Army was fighting as a racially integrated force. During 1951, the Army, to keep its units up to strength, was forced to implement individual rotation. Military historian Col. S. L. A. Marshall complained that "to my mind it was ruinous to morale and to good administrative order with an armed force. Whatever it gave the soldier, it sacrificed most of the traditional values, such as

Corporal Hiroshi N. Miyamura, *by George Akimoto, 1977. Corporal Miyamura of the 7th Infantry, 3d Infantry Division, repels Chinese soldiers during a night attack, 24–25 April 1951. Miyamura was subsequently captured and did not learn he had been awarded the Medal of Honor until his release in August 1953.*

earned promotion and citation, pride in unit and close comradeship, which are supposed to keep troops steadfast." Concern over the fighting qualities of American soldiers rose even further after the war, when about thirty-eight hundred returned from prisoner-of-war camps, bringing shocking reports of indiscipline, poor morale, and even collaboration. The Defense Department published a Code of Conduct for the "American fighting man" in 1955. The Communists were accused of "brainwashing" American soldiers, as sensationalized in a 1959 novel, *The Manchurian Candidate*, and the 1962 film of the same name.

In truth, the Army did not always fight well. Early in the war, some units and soldiers failed to successfully transition from a peacetime to a wartime mentality. Later in the war, leaders faced the difficult challenge of motivating their men in what was already being called the "forgotten war." At other times, units fought with great skill, such as the defense of Chipyong-ni in February 1951 by the 23d Infantry Regimental Combat Team reinforced by a French battalion. In the closing months of the war, the 7th Infantry

Division fought bravely to gain control of Pork Chop Hill, only to withdraw, rather than expend more lives unnecessarily before the armistice.

During the fighting, the U.S. Army rebuilt the Republic of Korea Army to over five hundred thousand strong. The U.S. military advisory group grew to about two thousand soldiers, who helped establish the Korean Army Training Center, reestablished the Korean Military Academy, and sent hundreds of Korean officers to military schools in the United States. Koreans provided direct support to U.S. forces with up to seventy-five thousand civilian laborers in the Korean Service Corps and about twenty-seven thousand Korean soldiers in the Korean Augmentation to the United States Army (KATUSA) program.

U.S. Army strength in the Far East grew to 247,000 soldiers in Korea, 108,000 in Japan, and 12,000 in the Ryukyu Islands. The Army fought in Korea with the doctrine, organization, and equipment of World War II. Innovations included body armor to protect against shell fragments and small-arms fire and an improved medical system that featured rapid casualty evacuation by helicopter, mobile army surgical hospitals, and a network of general hospitals in Japan, Okinawa, Hawaii, and the United States. When the 2.35-inch M9 Bazooka antitank rocket proved ineffective against the T34 tank, the Ordnance Corps rapidly fielded the 3.5-inch M20 Super Bazooka. The Army's mixed experience with unconventional warfare using anti-Communist partisans in the north led it to organize the U.S. Army Special Forces in 1952.

The Army faced enormous humanitarian challenges in the Korean War. During the first year, intense fighting and bombing swept the peninsula from north to south and created hundreds of thousands of refugees, often sick, injured, or starving. Refugees were caught in the crossfire, while political killings were common on both sides. Seoul changed hands four times. Villages, roads, and bridges were destroyed. Civil affairs loomed larger than ever before in the eyes of Army commanders.

The war of movement also generated large numbers of Chinese and Korean prisoners of war. The Army established prisoner-of-war camps on two islands: Koje-do and Cheju-do. By November 1950, their numbers swelled to one hundred thirty thousand. American and South Korean military police found it difficult to control the prisoners who staged riots, targeted killings, and disturbances inside the camps. In one such incident on Koje Island, Communists captured the camp commandant, a U.S. Army brigadier general, and held him hostage for four days. The United Nations Command eventually committed two American regimental combat teams and several allied units to regain control. The prisoner-of-war issue became a major stumbling block in the armistice negotiations, as well as a source of friction between the United States and its South Korean ally. At the end of the war, the United Nations Command repatriated 82,493 prisoners of war and the Communist forces returned 13,444 United Nations personnel.

To fight the war, the Army helped create a joint theater intelligence system. Army intelligence professionals created collection and analytic capabilities against North Korea, China, and Russia, including signals intelligence, prisoner-of-war interrogations, and translations. The Korean War was a "major milestone in the development of Army Intelligence," according to Army historian John Patrick Finnegan. "It revived intelligence capabilities which had grown moribund in the post–World War II retrenchment. It also witnessed the development of large-scale intelligence formations in the field." The Army sent elements of the 525th Military Intelligence Service Group to Korea to support field commanders and established the 500th Military Intelligence Service Group in Japan. In 1952, the Army's signals intelligence arm, the Army Security Agency, became part of the National Security Agency, with field stations in Japan, Okinawa, the Philippines, Hawaii, and Alaska. The new Central Intelligence Agency grew rapidly in the region.

The American public grew restless with the seemingly interminable stalemate. They followed the fighting in newspapers and by radio, especially if their sons were subject to the draft, but the news lacked the sweeping drama and bold victories of World War II. The 1952 presidential campaign was fought in part over Truman's policies in Korea. Eisenhower ran with a promise to go to Korea and end the war. Combined with Joseph Stalin's death in March 1953 and the general exhaustion of all parties to the conflict, a settlement was finally reached that July. American civilian and military leaders—other than the Army leadership—concluded that it was air power that had forced the Communists to sign an armistice, not ground troops. But Korea was essentially a ground war; the Army bore the brunt of American losses, including 27,731 soldiers killed in action.

THE NEW LOOK IN THE FAR EAST, 1953–1965

The Korean War occurred at a time of great turbulence in the region, as nationalist forces fought to overthrow western colonial power and postindependence governments sought to build new nations. The French fought one insurgency in Vietnam while the British fought another in Malaya. Many of the newly independent nations, including India and Indonesia, refused to align with either Cold War bloc. The United States built a framework for regional security that included mutual defense treaties with Australia and New Zealand, Japan, the Philippines, and the Republic of China (Taiwan), as well as South Korea. In 1954, the United States negotiated a Southeast Asia Collective Defense Treaty, although the Southeast Asia Treaty Organization (SEATO) never became an integrated military alliance like the North Atlantic Treaty Organization (NATO). After 1953, the Army poured resources into strengthening the armed forces of its regional partners: Japan, South Korea, Taiwan, the Philippines, and South Vietnam.

The war led the United States to dramatically increase its defense budgets, the size of its armed forces, and its research and development program. A consensus emerged among America's leaders and the public that the "Free World" was engaged in a global struggle with the Soviet Union. However, despite the "hot war" in Korea, most Americans considered Europe to be the most important arena of this struggle. During the 1950s, most senior Army leaders were veterans of World War II in Europe, not the Pacific. Of the twelve Army chiefs of staff who served in the thirty years after 1945, only four had served in the Pacific theater during World War II. Popular memory of the Pacific War emphasized the Navy and Marine Corps, such as the first major film documentary of the television age, *Victory at Sea*; the Iwo Jima Memorial in Arlington, Virginia; and the USS *Arizona* Memorial at Pearl Harbor. Nevertheless, the Korean War marked a rising generation of Army officers; of the next eleven Army chiefs of staff who served after 1953, all but two had served in Korea.

The Pacific Ocean became a Navy lake in another way, when the Defense Department inactivated FECOM in 1957, thus ending the division of the region between two commands. The Navy-led Pacific Command assumed responsibility for the entire region.

After the armistice, the Eighth Army was reduced to a single U.S. corps with two divisions standing watch along the demilitarized zone. The 1st Marine Division returned to the United States in 1955, after which the Army provided the only remaining American ground troops on the peninsula. By then, only sixty thousand American soldiers remained, mostly draftees on one-year tours, living in primitive field conditions in small posts. To deter aggression and counter the vast manpower reserves of North Korea and China, in 1958 the Army began to deploy atomic-capable systems to South Korea. These included the Honest John rocket, Nike-Hercules air defense missiles, 280-mm. cannon, and 8-inch howitzers. A U.S. Army general served as commander in chief of the United Nations Command, with command authority over all American, South Korean, and other United Nations forces, as well as joint commander of all U.S. forces. "Convoluted might be the kindest term describing the chain of command in Korea" during this period, wrote Daniel P. Bolger.

Korea remained a devastated land. The Army established the Korean Civil Assistance Command and the Armed Forces Assistance to Korea program, using military equipment and materiel for civilian relief and rehabilitation. Economic misery was compounded by political instability. In 1960–1961, founding president Syngman Rhee was ousted and Maj. Gen. Park Chung Hee established a military dictatorship.

In Japan, the Korean War brought an end to the occupation. The United States pressed the new Japanese government to arm itself against the Soviet threat, despite the Japanese constitution that explicitly prohibited military forces. Occupation authorities ordered Japan to establish a paramilitary National Police Reserve, which the Army helped expand to one hundred ten thousand personnel. On 8 September 1951, the United States and Japan signed a peace treaty and a mutual security treaty that ended the occupation on 28 April 1952. The U.S. Army continued to help Japan build its "ground self-defense forces" to about two hundred fifty thousand. The economic stimulus of Korean War spending put Japan on the path of rapid economic growth.

After 1953, the United States maintained substantial air and naval forces in Japan, but removed all ground combat forces. The 3d Marine Division arrived in Japan from the United States in 1953 but moved to Okinawa in 1956. In 1957, the 1st Cavalry Division in Japan transferred its colors to the 24th Infantry Division in Korea and was inactivated. When

FECOM was inactivated, the Air Force took command of all U.S. forces in Japan. U.S. Army, Japan, located at the former Imperial Japanese Army Academy at Camp Zama outside Tokyo, became the service component command. The Army maintained a large logistical, intelligence, and medical infrastructure in Japan, but by 1959, fewer than six thousand soldiers remained.

Okinawa became the keystone of U.S. air and land power in the region because of its strategic location and its legal status as an American protectorate. After the United States–Japan peace treaty, the United States established the U.S. Civil Administration of the Ryukyu Islands. Army lieutenant generals continued to serve as military governor until 1957, and after that, as high commissioner. In November 1956, the IX Corps headquarters transferred from Korea to Camp Buckner, Okinawa, where in January 1957 it merged with U.S. Army Ryukyus Command. In 1953, the Army Security Agency consolidated all signals intelligence activities on Okinawa at Kobe, renamed Torii Station in 1958. In the late 1950s the United States began to deploy atomic-capable systems to Okinawa. In June 1957, the Army activated the 1st Special Forces Group on Okinawa to prepare for unconventional warfare missions in China, Korea, and Indochina.

The Okinawan population recovered only slowly from the ravages of war, and the U.S. military remained a powerful presence in people's day-to-day lives. Between 1950 and 1957, the Army Corps of Engineers spent $300 million on the island to build military facilities, airfields, family housing, and infrastructure. In September 1956, the island was hit by the worst typhoon in living memory with winds up to 150 miles per hour. About 2,650 homes were completely destroyed and more than 4,000 severely damaged. The Army provided emergency relief and helped rebuild damaged infrastructure.

The United States had ended security assistance to Chinese Nationalist forces in late 1948, but with the outbreak of war in Korea, President Truman committed the United States to the defense of Taiwan. In May 1951, the United States established a military assistance advisory group. In 1954, the two Chinas seemed on the brink of war. The United States and the Republic of China signed a mutual defense treaty and the United States established the United States Taiwan Defense

Command, headed by an American vice admiral. The Army did not station any ground combat forces on Taiwan, but the Army Security Agency established a field station near Taipei.

In the Philippines, the center of America's pre-1941 regional defense strategy, the new government faced opposition from the Hukbalahaps, a Marxist-led peasant guerrilla army in central Luzon. In 1950, the United States expanded the Joint United States Military Assistance Group and assisted the government with a combination of military, economic, and psychological warfare measures. The Philippine government defeated the rebellion by 1955, much as the U.S. Army had defeated the Philippine guerrillas half a century earlier, by a mix of punitive and conciliatory measures. This success encouraged American military leaders to believe that success in counterinsurgency was possible, given the right strategy, a competent local government, and a limited commitment of resources.

In Indochina, where the French Army had been fighting since 1946 for control against Communist-led nationalists, the Viet Minh, the United States agreed to provide military assistance and in September 1950 established a military assistance advisory group in Saigon. In 1953, the Joint Chiefs of Staff sent the commander of U.S. Army, Pacific, Lt. Gen. John W. O'Daniel, on a military mission to Indochina, and he later assumed command of the advisory group. Late in 1953, the Viet Minh surrounded more than ten thousand French troops at Dien Bien Phu. The United States considered massive air strikes to break the siege, but General Ridgway, now the Army chief of staff, advised against relying on air power alone. Based on his experiences in Korea, he decried "the old delusive idea . . . that we could do things the cheap and easy way." President Dwight D. Eisenhower agreed and major U.S. assistance was withheld. On 7 May 1954, the French troops at Dien Bien Phu surrendered and France agreed to withdraw from Indochina. The United States took on responsibility to aid the new government of the Republic of Vietnam, established a training mission for the South Vietnamese Army, and began sending Vietnamese officers to military schools in the United States. By the late 1950s, the Army had over five hundred advisers stationed in that new country.

After 1953, Hawaii remained as important as ever to America's defense posture in the Pacific. In 1954, the 25th

Infantry Division moved from Korea to Schofield Barracks, and over the next several years, the Army developed the Pōhakuloa Training Area on the Island of Hawaii with 108,863 acres and built sixteen hundred family housing units on Oahu. After FECOM was inactivated, U.S. Army, Pacific, at Fort Shafter was elevated to the four-star level and became the service component command for all Army forces in the Asia-Pacific region.

Alaska remained vital, especially for North American air defense. The Army reinforced its defenses in 1951 with a regimental combat team mobilized from the South Dakota National Guard. The Army operated the Northern Warfare Training Center and in 1963 activated the 171st Infantry Brigade at Fort Wainwright and the 172d Infantry Brigade at Fort Richardson.

By 1959, when Congress approved statehood for Hawaii and Alaska, long-range aviation was transforming the strategic geography of the Asia-Pacific region. The Army was transforming itself in organization, doctrine, and equipment. The Army prepared to fight on an atomic battlefield, ready to deliver battlefield atomic weapons, if needed. It broke up its traditional regiments to form "pentomic" battle groups and began fielding a new generation of weapons systems in Hawaii and Korea, such as the M60 battle tank, M113 armored personnel carrier, UH–1 helicopter, and the 7.62-mm. M14 rifle. Rapidly advancing missile technology and the growing threat of long-range Soviet bombers caused the Army to turn to atomic-capable air defense systems. The Army deployed sophisticated air defense missile systems in Korea, Japan, Okinawa, and Hawaii. In 1958–1959, the Army Corps of Engineers built Nike-Hercules sites on Oahu, Okinawa, and Taiwan. In Hawaii, the Army National Guard assumed the antiaircraft mission.

Soldiers also supported nuclear weapons testing in the Marshall Islands and soon began testing missile defense technologies. In October 1957, the Soviet Union launched Sputnik, the first artificial satellite. Two years later, the U.S. Army Rocket and Guided Missile Agency selected Kwajalein Atoll in the Marshall Islands for a ballistic missile defense test site. The Army Corps of Engineers built a missile testing range on the remote atoll, and on 12 December 1962, a Nike-Zeus missile from Kwajalein successfully intercepted an intercontinental ballistic missile nose cone launched from Vandenberg Air Force Base, California. Nuclear weapons testing ended at the Pacific Proving Grounds when the United States signed the Partial Test Ban Treaty in 1963, but missile tests continued.

The John F. Kennedy administration came into office proclaiming a strategy of "flexible response," which gave greater weight to the Army and especially the Special Forces. At the same time, the Soviet Union declared support for "wars of national liberation." Yet the Korean War, wrote T. R. Fehrenbach in 1963, had "reaffirmed in American minds the distaste for land warfare on the continent of Asia." The United States responded to instability in Southeast Asia by deploying forces to Thailand, Laos, and South Vietnam. In 1961, the 7th Special Forces Group (Airborne) deployed mobile training teams to Laos in Operation WHITE STAR. In May 1962, the United States deployed a battle group from the 25th Infantry Division to Thailand, together with a Marine brigade, and established the U.S. Military Assistance Command, Thailand. In 1963, the Army activated the 173d Airborne Brigade on Okinawa as the quick-reaction force for Pacific Command and established a forward floating depot at Subic Bay in the Philippines with equipment for three battle groups. In 1964, the 25th Infantry Division tested the pre-positioning concept by sending units to a training exercise in Okinawa to link up with this materiel. Army divisions in Korea and Hawaii transformed under the Reorganization Objective Army Division (ROAD) design, which had a universal division structure with a variable number of maneuver brigades and combat battalions for different contingencies.

VIETNAM WAR, 1965–1973

By the early 1960s, the Republic of Vietnam was losing the battle against the Communist-led Viet Cong. U.S. Army personnel strength in South Vietnam increased to eleven thousand, and the Army deployed helicopters for battlefield mobility. In February 1962, Pacific Command established the Military Assistance Command, Vietnam (MACV), under General Paul D. Harkins, deputy commander of U.S. Army, Pacific. An adviser to a South Vietnamese infantry division, Lt. Col. John Paul Vann, admitted to reporters: "They're not the world's greatest fighters, . . . but they're good people, and they can win a war if someone shows them how." Special Forces soldiers trained and equipped Civilian Irregular Defense Group forces in the Central Highlands. Yet bad news continued to flow from the battlefields. In November 1963, the South Vietnamese Army overthrew the Saigon

CHINA

BURMA

CHINA

Red R

Black R

Dien Bien Phu

HANOI

LAOS

Mekong R

NORTH
VIETNAM

CHINA

HAINAN

Vinh

GULF
OF
TONKIN

VIENTIANE

Mekong R

THAILAND

DEMARCATION LINE

Quang Tri

Khe Sanh

Hue

Da Nang

My Lai

Ia Drang R

BANGKOK

Pleiku

Qui Nhon

CAMBODIA

SOUTH
VIETNAM

Tonle Sap

Mekong R

GULF
OF
THAILAND

Loc Ninh

Cam Ranh

PHNOM PENH

Tay Ninh

Bien Hoa

Long Binh

SAIGON

Dao Phu Quoc

Can Tho

SOUTH
CHINA
SEA

Con Son

SOUTHEAST ASIA
1965–1973

0   150

Miles

Map 4

regime, and after almost a decade of nation building the American project in South Vietnam teetered on the brink of failure. *(Map 4)*

In May 1964, MACV became a subunified command under General William C. Westmoreland, who had commanded the 187th Regimental Combat Team in Korea. MACV activated a joint unconventional warfare task force, the highly classified Studies and Observations Group (MACV-SOG), with about two thousand personnel, and the Army deployed the 5th Special Forces Group (Airborne) from Fort Bragg, North Carolina. The Navy began an aggressive patrolling program against North Vietnam, and in August 1964 U.S. and North Vietnamese naval vessels clashed in the Gulf of Tonkin. In response, the U.S. Congress authorized President Lyndon B. Johnson "to take all necessary measures to repel any armed attack against the forces of the United States and to prevent further aggression," and to assist South Vietnam "in defense of its freedom." In February 1965, the Air Force and Navy began a sustained bombing campaign to interdict soldiers and materiel sent from the north. In March, President Johnson sent ground combat units into South Vietnam to defend air bases and stabilize the situation. The 9th Marines deployed from Okinawa and the Philippines to defend the airfield at Da Nang. The 173d Airborne Brigade deployed from Okinawa to secure an air base at Bien Hoa northeast of Saigon, followed by the 2d Brigade, 1st Infantry Division, from Fort Riley, Kansas; the 1st Brigade, 101st Airborne Division, from Fort Campbell, Kentucky; and the 1st Cavalry Division (Airmobile) from Fort Benning, Georgia.

The first major clash between American and North Vietnamese units came in November 1965, when a brigade of the 1st Cavalry Division air-assaulted into the Central Highlands into the midst of three regiments of the *People's Army of Vietnam*. When the enemy attacked the 1st and 2d Battalions, 7th Cavalry, the Americans fought back with everything they had but took heavy casualties. The battle demonstrated the airmobile concept, but more importantly the valor and skill of the American soldier.

During 1965 and 1966, the Army poured combat and support units into South Vietnam. The Marine Corps deployed the III Marine Amphibious Force to the northern provinces with two Marine divisions. In December 1965, the 25th Infantry Division began to deploy from Hawaii. In September 1966, the 11th Armored Cavalry arrived and was equipped with the pre-positioned materiel stored afloat in the Philippines. In July 1965, the Army established U.S. Army, Vietnam, and the

1st Logistical Command to support the Army, other services, and allied forces throughout the country. U.S. Army Engineer Command, Vietnam, supervised thousands of soldiers, civilians, and contractors to create the infrastructure to support a massive effort in the undeveloped country.

The war was devastating to the Vietnamese people, millions of whom became refugees. American soldiers often scorned Vietnamese as "gooks," but also conducted extensive humanitarian assistance and civic action programs to win "hearts and minds" and encourage support for the Saigon regime. As had happened in Korea, the internecine guerrilla war and the presence of foreign soldiers in large numbers inevitably distorted Vietnam's society, culture, and economy.

The U.S. Army in Vietnam was led by senior officers and noncommissioned officers, many of whom were Korean War veterans. Most junior officers were commissioned through the Reserve Officers' Training Corps or Officer Candidate School. To train junior noncommissioned officers, the Army established twelve-week noncommissioned officer candidate schools. Despite rising manpower requirements, President Johnson increased draft calls rather than call up the National Guard or Reserves. As in Korea, the Army used individual replacements to keep units up to strength, rather than rotating units, and officers rotated to noncombat assignments after six months. As a result, wrote historian Ronald H. Spector, "the Army was faced with the problem of endemic personnel turbulence occasioned by the very high turnover rates made necessary by the twelve-month tour."

The American soldier's experience in Vietnam varied greatly depending on time and place. Most served on large firebases in support functions. Soldiers absorbed a torrent of new technology during the war, including helicopters, armored personnel carriers, body armor, tactical and strategic communications, and automatic data processing systems. Soldiers in combat units faced a tenacious foe in an unforgiving environment. Novelist Tim O'Brien, himself a Vietnam veteran, has one character express irritation when people said "how special Nam is, how it's a big aberration in the history of American wars—how for the soldier it's somehow different from Korea or World War Two. Follow me? I'm saying that the *feel* of war is the same in Nam or Okinawa—the emotions are the same, the same fundamental stuff is seen and remembered."

Soldiers of the 1st Squadron, 9th Cavalry, 1st Cavalry Division (Airmobile), air assault into a hilltop position in Quang Ngai Province, April 1967.

The United States brought in allies through the Free World Assistance Program, informally known as Many Flags. Several key regional allies joined in the fight. The Republic of Korea sent two infantry divisions and one marine brigade, which served under independent command. Thailand sent a division. Australia sent a brigade-size task force. New Zealand sent two rifle companies and a 105-mm. howitzer battery. The Philippines sent a civic action group of engineers and medical personnel.

While the United States was engaged in Vietnam, instability continued to threaten the rest of the region. In Korea, the I Corps included the 7th Infantry Division and the 2d Infantry Division (reflagged from the 1st Cavalry Division in 1965). North Korean leader Kim Il Sung launched commando raids and probing attacks across the Demilitarized Zone, captured the USS *Pueblo*, an unarmed U.S. Navy intelligence-collection vessel off its coast, and shot down a U.S. Navy EC–121 intelligence-collection aircraft over international waters. U.S. and South Korean soldiers fought a low-intensity conflict along the Demilitarized Zone. American units suffered from personnel shortages, a lack of funding, and sagging morale.

Street Scene, *by Kenneth J. Scowcroft, 1967*

Elsewhere in the region, the United States stepped up military assistance. In the Philippines, two armed opposition groups developed in the late 1960s, the Maoist New People's Army and the Moro National Liberation Front in the Muslim south. After a military regime in Indonesia destroyed the Communist Party in 1965–1966, the United States resumed military-to-military contacts, and the 1st Special Forces Group began teaching the Indonesian Army how to conduct civic action programs.

In South Vietnam, American and South Vietnamese forces took the offensive by the fall of 1966. Allied forces simultaneously fought a guerrilla war and a big unit war. Like the Korean War, the Vietnam War was not fought for terrain or military victory, but for limited political objectives. U.S. officials ramped up the "other war," pulling together all support to pacification in a unique organization, Civil Operations and Revolutionary Development Support (CORDS), under the direction of a civilian MACV deputy commander.

By early 1968, American combat involvement had already lasted as long as the Korean War, with no end in sight. American civilian and military leaders remained publicly optimistic about the war's progress, but privately expressed growing concerns. In

January 1968, with U.S. troop strength over half a million, intelligence indicators pointed towards a Communist offensive. The commander of II Field Force in Long Binh, Lt. Gen. Frederick C. Weyand, responded by repositioning his forces to better protect Saigon. On 30 January 1968, the Communist offensive began during the Tet new year's holiday truce. American and South Vietnamese forces recovered from their initial surprise and over several weeks dealt a crushing defeat to the attackers, killing an estimated fifty-eight thousand and destroying the local Viet Cong infrastructure. The U.S. Army lost almost four thousand killed in action and the South Vietnamese Army almost five thousand. President Johnson finally authorized a limited mobilization of the reserve components, including the 29th Infantry Brigade (Hawaii Army National Guard) and 100th Battalion, 442d Infantry (Army Reserve), many of whose soldiers served in Vietnam as individual replacements.

American search-and-destroy tactics, combined with heavy fire power, raised dilemmas of waging war with civilians nearby, and on occasion American soldiers committed atrocities. The most notorious such incident occurred on 16 March 1968, when a platoon from the 11th Infantry Brigade on a search-and-destroy mission wantonly killed as many as five hundred villagers at My Lai. When the incident came to light, the Army Criminal Investigation Division investigated and the Army chief of staff convened a three-star board of inquiry. The platoon leader, 1st Lt. William L. Calley Jr., was convicted by court-martial and sentenced to life in prison. He served three years.

Although the Tet offensive was an allied battlefield victory, it caused the American people to rethink their open-ended support for the war. President Johnson announced he would not run for reelection, halted the bombing of the north, and initiated peace talks with the North Vietnamese. Westmoreland returned to the United States to become Army chief of staff. His replacement, General Creighton W. Abrams, had spent the previous year working to build the South Vietnamese Army. That same year, Americans had other concerns beyond Vietnam. In April 1968, American cities erupted in anger after the assassination of civil rights leader Rev. Martin Luther King Jr. The 1968 presidential campaign was tumultuous. The Republican candidate, Richard M. Nixon, hinted that he had a plan to end the war, just as President Eisenhower had promised to end the Korean War, and upon taking office he sought "peace with honor."

Nevertheless the war continued, as did the interminable peace talks in Paris. After Tet, Abrams placed increased emphasis on Vietnamization and pacification. By 1970, the United States assigned more than fourteen thousand advisers, 90 percent of whom were provided by the Army, to South Vietnamese units. In April 1969, at the peak of its involvement, the United States had some 543,000 military personnel in Vietnam, with many thousands more stationed throughout the region in Thailand, Okinawa, Japan, and Hawaii. President Nixon announced a phased withdrawal of U.S. forces from Vietnam and the "Guam Doctrine," by which the United States would rely on South Vietnamese forces, and regional partners more broadly, to bear the burden of security with only indirect American support. He announced that America would no longer prepare to fight two wars simultaneously, but only one-and-a-half wars. By implication, the half war would be in Asia.

Despite Nixon's efforts, public support in America continued to erode and the antiwar movement gathered strength. On 27 June 1969, *Life Magazine* shocked the nation by publishing the photographs of one week's toll, the pictures of 242 young Americans killed from 28 May to 3 June 1969. Under pressure of a lengthy

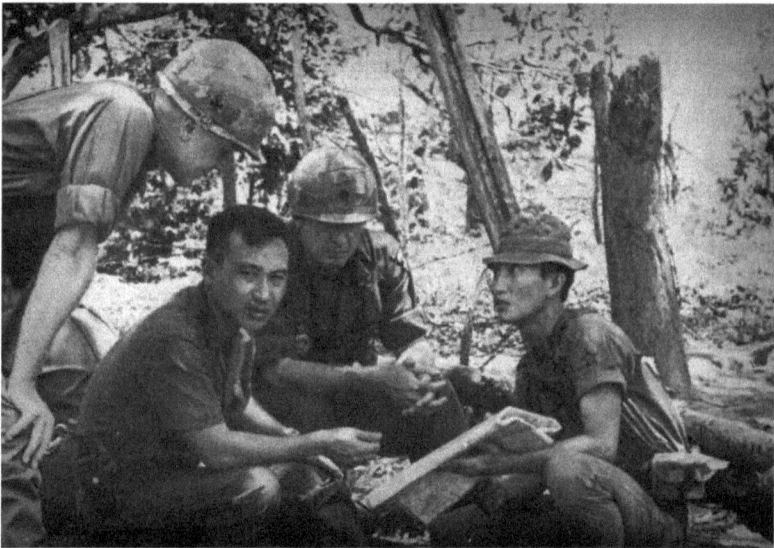

American officers coach their South Vietnamese counterparts during a combat operation, 1969–1970.

and unpopular war, elements of the draftee Army slid into insubordination, racial tension, and drug abuse. Professional officers and noncommissioned officers faced the strain of multiple combat tours. By early 1970, senior Army leaders expressed concern that the prospect of sending officers back for a third one-year tour was causing too many to resign their commissions.

Nixon sought to regain the initiative with bold action. In the spring of 1970, he sent the U.S. Army and South Vietnamese Army across the border into Cambodia to disrupt Communist forces in what had been an off-limits sanctuary, but U.S. Army involvement in combat operations was drawing down. The 101st Airborne Division began the last major U.S. combat operation on 5 September 1970. In February 1971, the division also supported the South Vietnamese Operation LAM SON 719 across the border into Laos with helicopter and artillery support, but no ground troops or advisers.

In the spring of 1971, the III Marine Amphibious Force left for Okinawa with the last Marine ground combat units. The 101st Airborne Division remained until January 1972. In the spring of 1972, the North Vietnamese launched a conventional invasion of the south, but the South Vietnamese, with the support of U.S. air power and logistical support, seemed able to defend themselves. That June, the Army withdrew its last two infantry brigades, the 3d Brigade, 1st Cavalry Division, and the 196th Infantry Brigade. By 30 November 1972, only 16,100 Army personnel remained. After intense U.S. bombing raids against the north in December 1972, an armistice was signed in Paris that took effect on 28 January 1973 and allowed the Army to complete its withdrawal, leaving only a small defense attaché office in Saigon. The Army had suffered over thirty thousand killed in action. Many were laid to rest in the Punchbowl in Hawaii alongside casualties of World War II and the Korean War.

AFTER VIETNAM, 1973 TO PRESENT

RESTORING CONFIDENCE, 1973–1991

The South Vietnamese government endured for two years after the U.S. Army departed, but when the North attacked again in April 1975, the war-weary Congress failed to provide any more support. The U.S. Congress had ended the draft, restricted presidential war-making powers, and slashed aid to South Vietnam. President Nixon resigned in August 1974 during the Watergate scandal, further weakening America's commitment to enforcing the Paris Peace Accords. America's withdrawal from Vietnam was part of a general American drawdown in the region. Nixon withdrew the I Corps and the 7th Infantry Division from Korea in 1971 and in 1972 inactivated the 171st Infantry Brigade at Fort Wainwright, Alaska. The United States returned Okinawa to Japan in 1972. Japan allowed the United States to continue to station forces on Okinawa, but the United States had to withdraw all nuclear weapons. In 1974, the Army inactivated U.S. Army, Pacific. The Eighth Army in Korea and U.S. Army, Japan, became independent major commands that reported directly to Headquarters, Department of the Army.

In early 1975, North Vietnam launched a final offensive that more resembled the North Korean attack on South Korea in 1950 than the guerrilla tactics of the previous twenty years. Congress

73

would approve the use of U.S. troops only for the evacuation of U.S. citizens. "The Americans could provide money and weapons," concluded historian George C. Herring, "but they could not furnish the ingredients necessary for political stability and military success." With little American support, the South Vietnamese Army collapsed and Saigon fell on 1 May 1975. In Cambodia, the Khmer Rouge established a violent dictatorship until a Vietnamese invasion drove them from power in 1979. Thailand stood alone as a bulwark against communism in Southeast Asia but ordered all American forces to withdraw and established full diplomatic relations with Hanoi. The Army sent two thousand support troops to Guam, where they set up a tent city for more than fifty thousand Indochinese refugees, eventually helping process over one hundred twelve thousand. In the United States, the Army established refugee centers at Fort Chaffee, Arkansas, and Fort Indiantown Gap, Pennsylvania, which together housed over seventy-two thousand.

The strategic geography of the Asia-Pacific region was shifting. Once the arena of great-power rivalry, now no external power could exercise much influence. Britain had announced in 1968 that it would withdraw its remaining troops from "east of Suez," primarily Malaysia and Singapore, except for a garrison in Hong Kong. France retained only token forces in the South Pacific. SEATO dissolved in 1977, leaving in its place the Association of Southeast Asian Nations, which excluded the United States and was not a collective security organization.

China increased its influence in the region. A border conflict with the Soviet Union in 1969 made it impossible to speak any longer of a monolithic Communist threat. President Nixon began a rapprochement in 1971 that reduced the risk of military confrontation. When Deng Xiaoping came to power in 1977, he put an end to the Cultural Revolution and announced a major reform program known as the Four Modernizations that put China on a path towards rapid economic growth. China seemed to focus on its domestic agenda, but attacked its former ally, Vietnam, in 1979 and remained a strategic threat with a small nuclear arsenal and ballistic missiles that could reach Hawaii and the West Coast. In 1979, the United States switched its diplomatic recognition to the People's Republic of China and ended military assistance to Taiwan. Although sales of military supplies and equipment to Taiwan continued, the United States Taiwan

Defense Command was inactivated and the mutual defense treaty was terminated.

Some countries experienced unprecedented growth. Japan, South Korea, Hong Kong, and Taiwan became known as the Four Tigers for their rapid, export-driven industrial growth. Other countries, many of them nondemocratic and unstable—such as China, Indonesia, Cambodia, and Malaysia—recovered slowly from internal unrest or civil wars. In 1986, the "People Power" movement overthrew an authoritarian regime in the Philippines, but the Maoist New People's Army remained active and on 21 April 1989 assassinated U.S. Army Col. James N. Rowe, who was assigned to the Joint U.S. Military Advisory Group.

The Vietnam War had a lasting effect on the Army as an institution. All its senior leaders had served in Vietnam, including every Army chief of staff until 2003. The war's bitter end was a painful personal loss for all the soldiers who had served there. The Army turned away to rebuild Seventh Army in Europe while still preparing for limited contingencies in Southwest Asia. Army leaders reoriented doctrine and training towards high-intensity conventional operations in Central Europe, as had occurred during the October 1973 war in the Middle East. In 1976, U.S. Army Training and Doctrine Command published a new Field Manual 100–5, *Operations*, that was explicitly focused on defending Central Europe against the superior numbers of the Warsaw Pact. "The part of the Army configured for the main battle of Central Europe," wrote RAND analyst Carl H. Builder in 1989, "is, I think, the mainstream Army—that is its first love and priority."

As the Army became an all-volunteer force, Congress increased military pay and benefits and funded quality-of-life improvements, but it still faced difficulties in recruiting and a decline in the overall quality of recruits. It opened more Army specialties to women and sent more of them overseas. The number of female soldiers stationed in Korea rose from 20 in 1972 to 1,593 in 1978.

Under the new Total Force policy, the Army assigned National Guard brigades to active divisions. The 25th Infantry Division was reactivated in 1972 at Schofield Barracks with only two active brigades. The 29th Infantry Brigade of the Hawaii Army National Guard was assigned as its "round-out" brigade. The Army began the CAPSTONE program in 1979 to align other reserve component units with their wartime chain of command, and in 1981 the Army began using reserve component soldiers on short tours under the Overseas Deployment Training Program.

The Korean Peninsula remained volatile as the U.S. Army struggled to rebuild its units there. Most soldiers served unaccompanied one-year tours and were housed in the austere conditions of a combat zone. Lt. Col. Colin L. Powell, who served two tours in Vietnam, took command of an infantry battalion in Korea in 1973 and faced daunting challenges of indiscipline, drug abuse, and racial tension. Off-base, soldiers were seen as a source of crimes such as drug trafficking and prostitution.

Nevertheless, the Army strengthened its leadership and upgraded its capabilities on the peninsula. The 2d Infantry Division deployed advanced weapons systems that the South Korean Army did not have, such as the TOW antitank missile, AH–1 Cobra attack helicopter, and in the mid-1980s, the AH–64 Apache attack helicopter. In the mid-1970s, the Army replaced Honest John and Sergeant missiles with dual-capable Lance missiles with a range of up to seventy-eight miles. Army logisticians with the 19th Support Command created the Army Pre-positioned Stock-4 at Camp Carroll with equipment for an armored brigade.

Pacific Command maintained Operation Plan 5027 for the defense of Korea, which called for massive reinforcement from the United States. In 1976, the United States and South Korea began Exercise TEAM SPIRIT to show their resolve. That same year, North Korean guards unexpectedly attacked a U.S. Army party trimming a tree in the Joint Security Area at Panmunjom, killing a U.S. captain and wounding several other U.S. and South Korean personnel. The United States and South Korea responded with Operation PAUL BUNYAN, a powerful show of force.

Despite such incidents, President Jimmy Carter announced a total withdrawal of U.S. forces in 1977. The chief of staff of U.S. Forces, Korea, Maj. Gen. John K. Singlaub, was quoted in the *Washington Post* as saying: "If U.S. ground troops are withdrawn on the schedule suggested, it will lead to war." Carter ordered his relief, but apparently the controversy had an effect. The president halted the withdrawal before all U.S. forces were removed. The 2d Infantry Division remained as a tripwire force.

In 1978, the United States and Republic of Korea established the binational Combined Forces Command that was distinct from United Nations Command and did not fall under U.S. Pacific Command. United States Forces Korea and Eighth Army continued much as before. In 1979, a military coup overthrew the South Korean government, and the next year the new government violently suppressed an uprising in Kwangju, killing hundreds of protesters. Many Koreans were angered at the United States for tacitly condoning the killings because the Korean forces involved were assumed to have been under the control of Combined Forces Command. Yet the contrast between the north and south was still clear. While Seoul prepared to host the 1988 Summer Olympic Games, North Korea became an active state sponsor of terrorism. It attempted to assassinate the South Korean president and his entire cabinet while on a state visit to Burma (the president escaped, but the blast killed four cabinet officers and two senior presidential advisers), and in 1987 it planted a bomb on a Korean Airlines flight, killing 115.

The United States was also concerned that the Soviet Union would take advantage of its withdrawal from Asia. In 1979, the Soviet navy established a base in Vietnam at the former American military port of Cam Ranh Bay with about twenty-five ships and nearly forty aircraft. In Northeast Asia opposing forces remained on a hair trigger. U.S. forces remained nuclear-capable throughout this period as a deterrent against other regional nuclear powers. American leaders still perceived nuclear weapons to have tactical utility for countering massed land formations, for air defense, and for striking command and control facilities. When a commercial airliner flying from Anchorage to Seoul strayed over the Kamchatka Peninsula on 1 September 1983, the Soviet air defenses, thinking it was an American reconnaissance aircraft, destroyed it, killing all 269 passengers and crew, including U.S. Congressman Lawrence P. McDonald (D-Georgia). Cold War tensions rose to a fever pitch, but tensions eased in 1986 when a new Soviet leader, Mikhail S. Gorbachev, traveled to Vladivostok to announce a new era of Soviet engagement with the Asia-Pacific region.

The United States took a renewed interest in South Asia and the Indian Ocean after the India-Pakistan war of 1971. On 1 January 1972, the secretary of defense assigned to Pacific Command responsibility for the countries of southern Asia and much of the Indian Ocean, and the U.S. Navy built an airfield and communications station on the remote British territory of Diego Garcia. In 1980, the Army stationed the Army Pre-positioned Stock-3 afloat there with equipment for an armored brigade.

The Army continued to rebuild and modernize in the region by engaging in a number of construction and facilities improvement programs. From 1975 to 1979, the Army Corps of Engineers oversaw construction of a $113 million, 2,600-unit joint-service housing project on Oahu in the former ammunition storage depot in the Aliamanu Crater, which one historian has called "the largest family housing development ever attempted by the Corps of Engineers." In 1976, in order to tell the story of the Army in Hawaii and the Asia-Pacific, U.S. Army Support Command, Hawaii, opened the U.S. Army Museum of Hawaii in a former coast artillery emplacement at Fort DeRussy. In Japan, the Japanese government began the Japan Facilities Improvement Program in 1979 for military construction, especially family housing and community support facilities. Also in 1979, the Army activated U.S. Army Western Command at Fort Shafter. In 1980, Army signals intelligence activities moved into a renovated World War II–era underground facility at Wheeler Field, which became Field Station Kunia.

The Army in the Asia-Pacific region benefited from President Ronald W. Reagan's defense buildup in the early 1980s. The secretary of defense, Caspar W. Weinberger, had served as a 41st Infantry Division platoon leader on New Guinea in 1943. Weinberger later wrote that he was "proud to have served in the infantry, and even given the vastly different situation of the 1980s, I knew the infantry was and is still the infantry. Without it and its ability to take and hold enemy ground, we would never be able to win wars." In 1985, the 25th Infantry Division expanded to include a third active infantry brigade and transformed into a light infantry division.

Alaska grew in importance with the discovery of oil at Prudhoe Bay in 1968 and the completion of the Trans-Alaska Pipeline in 1977. The Army activated the 6th Infantry Division (Light) at Fort Richardson in 1986, absorbing the 172d Infantry Brigade and adding a second active brigade. The 81st Infantry Brigade of the Washington Army National Guard became its round-out brigade.

The Goldwater-Nichols Act of 1986 expanded the importance of joint operations and the authority of combatant commanders, such as Pacific Command. The Army increasingly supported joint and special operations activities. Pacific Command established Special Operations Command Pacific in 1983 at Camp H. M. Smith, and in 1984 the Army reactivated the 1st Special Forces Group (Airborne), with one battalion at Torii Station, Okinawa, and two at Fort Lewis, Washington.

Men of the 1st Battalion, 23d Infantry, 3d Brigade, 2d Infantry Division, with M2A1 Bradley fighting vehicles and M1A1 Abrams tanks in the Twin Bridges Maneuver Area, South Korea, November 1998. The soldiers deployed from Fort Lewis, Washington, for Exercise FOAL EAGLE.

These new capabilities were well suited to the new emphasis on military-to-military engagement. Western Command began the Expanded Relations Program in 1978 with annual Pacific Armies Management Seminars and a slate of bilateral training exercises. In the early 1980s, the United States began a series of bilateral exercises with several countries, such as Exercise COBRA GOLD with Thailand and Exercise YAMA SAKURA with Japan.

AFTER THE COLD WAR, 1991–2001

In Europe, 1989 brought dramatic changes; in the Asia-Pacific region, the end of the Cold War was less notable. China's rulers suppressed prodemocracy demonstrators in Tiananmen Square in June 1989. Longer-term trends in the region ultimately had greater impact than the end of the global superpower confrontation. Democracy blossomed in South Korea, Taiwan, the Philippines, and Indonesia. Standards of living rose and dozens of cities swelled into enormous urban conglomerations, including several where the U.S. Army had fought or been stationed in years past: Shanghai, Beijing, Tokyo, Seoul, Jakarta, and Manila. The British colony of Hong Kong peacefully reverted to China in 1997. Economies steadily became more connected to the global economy, although the downside of this became evident when the region plunged into a severe financial crisis in 1997–1998. The United States became ever more dependent on raw materials and finished products from the region, especially from China. Countries in the region adopted the Internet with astonishing speed. Russia withdrew from the region to concentrate on its internal problems and the Russian Navy left Cam Ranh Bay. The wars of the past century seemed a distant memory, with one exception.

On the Korean Peninsula, the Cold War continued as North Korea slid into prolonged crisis. China and Russia reduced the aid that had long propped up the regime. Kim Il Sung died in 1994 and the country suffered flooding and a severe famine. Yet, North Korea continued to be a formidable military threat. In 1998, it fired a ballistic missile over Japanese territory and developed the capability to span the Pacific as far as America's West Coast. South Korea and the United States kept their military forces in readiness but also sought to reduce tensions. In 1991, President George H. W. Bush announced the withdrawal of all nuclear weapons from the region. The Army also withdrew its stocks of chemical weapons and destroyed them in the Johnston Atoll Chemical Agent Disposal System from 1990 to 2000. The 2d Infantry Division inactivated its third brigade in 1992. South Korea and the United States suspended Exercise TEAM SPIRIT in 1993 and the U.S. Army pulled back from the Demilitarized Zone. At the same time, to increase its combat power on the peninsula, the Army deployed the 6th Cavalry Brigade with attack helicopters and sent Patriot surface-to-air missiles.

Meanwhile, the United States had shifted its attention to Southwest Asia. The hundred-hour victory over Iraq in the final ground phase in Operation DESERT STORM in 1991 was a far cry from the three years of the Korean War or the ten years of the Vietnam War. President Bush boasted: "By God, we've kicked the Vietnam syndrome once and for all." By that time, the Army had already begun drawing on its forces in the Asia-Pacific region for contingencies elsewhere. The 7th Infantry Division (Light) at Fort Ord, California, long apportioned to the Korean contingency, was sent to Panama in December 1989. In early 1995, the

25th Infantry Division (Light) at Schofield Barracks, Hawaii, deployed to Haiti for peacekeeping duties.

Even with the victory against Iraq, Army Chief of Staff General Gordon R. Sullivan was concerned about readiness in an era of declining budgets and proliferating missions. To remind the Army of the costs of unpreparedness, he reached back to the Korean War. In many of his speeches, he would state clearly that on his watch there would be "No more Task Force Smiths!"

Within the region, the Army became involved in multinational peacekeeping missions. In the wake of civil war in Cambodia, it supported the United Nations Transitional Authority in Cambodia (UNTAC), led by an Australian general, while Special Operations Forces soldiers conducted humanitarian demining operations in Cambodia, Laos, Thailand, and Vietnam. In 1992, the Defense Department formed Joint Task Force–Full Accounting, which included the U.S. Army Central Identification Laboratory–Hawaii (established in 1976), to identify the remains of U.S. service personnel missing in action in Southeast Asia. The joint task force even opened a detachment in Hanoi. In 1995, the Defense Department opened the Asia-Pacific Center for Security Studies on Fort DeRussy in Honolulu.

Pacific Command stepped up its military-to-military engagements in the region. In 1992, Special Operations Command Pacific started the Joint/Combined Exchange Training Program. However, engagement became more difficult with some countries. The Philippines let U.S. basing rights expire in 1991, which forced the U.S. Navy and Air Force to close their long-time facilities, but approved a new bilateral training series, Exercise BALIKATAN. In 1992, the U.S. Congress suspended security cooperation with Indonesia after Indonesian security forces shot and killed civilian demonstrators in East Timor. U.S. Army, Pacific, expanded its senior-leader engagement program with the Pacific Armies Chiefs Conference, a biannual event that started in 1999 in Singapore and was attended by Army Chief of Staff General Eric K. Shinseki. Born in Hawaii, he was the first U.S. Army general of Japanese descent. His uncles had served in World War II in the 100th Infantry Battalion and 442d Regimental Combat Team; he had graduated from the U.S. Military Academy and had served and been wounded in Vietnam.

Soldiers also supported numerous humanitarian operations. On 11 September 1992, Typhoon Iniki struck the island of Kauai,

Hawaii. U.S. Army, Pacific, activated Joint Task Force–Hawaii to organize relief with 2,900 active-duty soldiers, 1,800 National Guardsmen, and 1,900 sailors and marines. The Army used two logistics support vessels based at Pearl Harbor, *Maj. Gen. Charles P. Gross* (LSV–5) and *CW3 Harold C. Clinger* (LSV–2). When an earthquake struck Kobe, Japan, on 17 January 1995, killing about 6,400, the logisticians of U.S. Army, Japan, provided rapid assistance. Soldiers provided similar support for other natural disasters around the Ring of Fire, a belt that girds the Pacific in which large numbers of earthquakes and volcanic eruptions occur. These included the earthquake and tsunami that struck in the Indian Ocean on 26 December 2004 and killed over two hundred thousand, and the earthquake and tsunami that hit Fukushima, Japan, on 11 March 2011, which left almost twenty thousand dead or missing.

In 1999, when violence erupted in East Timor (Timor-Leste) between the Indonesia military and independence forces, the United Nations Security Council authorized the International Force for East Timor (INTERFET), which was led by Australia. U.S. Army, Pacific, deployed the U.S. Support Group East Timor with up to two thousand personnel to provide logistics and communications support. For the first time in the region, the Army used the Logistics Civil Augmentation Program (LOGCAP) in support of the United Nations operations in East Timor for a broad range of logistics and support services to U.S. and allied forces. Army Materiel Command awarded the first contract to DynCorp in 1997 and in 2001 a follow-on contract to Kellogg, Brown & Root Services.

Other threats were less obvious. In January 1995, Manila police stumbled on a plot to place bombs on eleven airliners headed for the United States. The ringleader, Khalid Sheikh Mohammed, eluded capture and set about planning to use airliners for even more effective attacks against the United States. On 23 March 1995, a Japanese religious sect, Aum Shinrikyo attacked the Tokyo subway system with sarin nerve gas in an attempt to spread panic and terror by causing mass casualties. Their plan misfired, but they killed thirteen and severely injured fifty. The world was learning that nonstate actors could create as much havoc as state-sponsored terrorists.

THE ASIA-PACIFIC IN THE AGE OF TERROR, 2001–2012

When al-Qaeda attacked the United States on 11 September 2001, U.S. forces stationed in the Asia-Pacific region went on high alert. The suspension of air traffic reminded everyone of the region's interdependence and vulnerabilities in the era of "just-in-time" manufacturing and the military's reliance on power projection from the continental United States. Pacific Command designated U.S. Army, Pacific, as the Joint Rear Area Coordinator–Hawaii and it prepared to protect military and civilian assets in Hawaii. The task force soon grew into Joint Task Force–Homeland Defense, responsible also for Guam, American Samoa, and other territories in the South Pacific. When Northern Command was activated in 2002 for homeland defense, Pacific Command retained responsibility for Hawaii and its Army component, U.S. Army, Pacific, remained involved in local joint and interagency coordination to a greater extent than most Army commands in the continental United States.

Since the mid-1990s, the United States had been concerned about terrorist groups operating within the region. In 1997, the U.S. State Department had named the Abu Sayyaf Group in the southern Philippines as a terrorist organization for its persistent bombings and kidnappings. On 30 December 2000, another terrorist group, suspected to be the Moro Islamic Liberation Front, exploded a bomb outside the U.S. embassy in Manila, injuring nine. On 27 May 2001, the Abu Sayyaf Group kidnapped sixteen people on Palawan Island, including three Americans. In addition to threats to its officials and citizens, the United States had broader concerns about possible regional, and perhaps even worldwide, links among radical Islamist groups.

When Pacific Command began Operation ENDURING FREEDOM in the Philippines, Special Operations Command Pacific activated Joint Task Force 510. The commander of 1st Special Forces Group (Airborne) activated Army Special Operations Task Force–Philippines. In conjunction with Exercise BALIKATAN 02-01, about six hundred U.S. military personnel deployed to the southern Philippines in February 2002, of whom up to 160 deployed to Basilan Island. The 10th Area Support Group in Japan assumed the logistical support mission. The task force suffered its first casualties on 21 February 2002 in the crash of a MH–47E that killed eight soldiers and two airmen. U.S. soldiers had waged counterinsurgency in this area one hundred years earlier. According to journalist Robert D. Kaplan, who visited the southern Philippines in 2003, "in historical terms America had come full circle."

Violent extremists struck in Indonesia as well. On 12 October 2002, Jemaah Islamiyah exploded a vehicle-borne bomb that killed 202 and injured 240 others in a tourist spot on Bali, and on 5 August 2003, bombed a JW Marriott hotel in Jakarta. The United States and its allies were engaged in what appeared to be a global insurgency. Much of what the Army knew about insurgencies had been learned over the previous century in the Asia-Pacific region.

When the United States struck back in Afghanistan, the source of the attacks on 11 September 2001, nations throughout the region contributed forces, including Australia and New Zealand. Others cooperated closely with the United States, each in its own way. When the United States and Britain attacked Iraq to remove a suspected nuclear threat, several long-term partner nations in the region joined the international coalition, including Australia, Japan, New Zealand, the Philippines, Thailand, and Tonga. The Republic of Korea committed two infantry brigades.

Over the next several years, active and reserve component forces from Alaska, Hawaii, Guam, and South Korea deployed to Afghanistan, Iraq, and the Horn of Africa as part of the global force pool and the Army Force Generation process. In 2004, Headquarters, 25th Infantry Division (Light), went to Afghanistan and took over the mission as Combined Joint Task Force–76 with nearly thirteen thousand U.S. personnel and forces from eighteen coalition nations. In 2005, the 172d Infantry Brigade at Fort Richardson, Alaska, which had replaced the last active brigade of the 6th Infantry Division, transformed into a Stryker brigade combat team, deployed to Iraq, and on its return, was reflagged as the 1st Brigade Combat Team, 25th Infantry Division. The 1st Battalion, 501st Infantry (Airborne), at Fort Wainwright became the nucleus for the 4th Infantry Brigade Combat Team, 25th Infantry Division. Other units deployed for previous commitments. In early 2002, the 25th Infantry Division (Light) deployed more than two thousand soldiers as part of the NATO Stabilization Force in Bosnia-Herzegovina.

While the Army continued these operations, it also transformed how it managed its installations. In 2002, the U.S. Army Installation Management Agency (renamed Installation Management Command in 2006) created regional headquarters in Hawaii and Korea that took over garrison functions from the senior mission commanders. The two regions merged in 2011.

Soldiers of the 1st Battalion, 5th Infantry, 1st Brigade Combat Team, 25th Infantry Division, train Philippine Army troops at Fort Ramon Magsaysay, February 2008. The U.S. soldiers deployed from Fort Wainwright, Alaska, to the Philippines for Exercise BALIKATAN.

The confrontation in Korea continued after 2001, as North Korea rejected international calls to halt its nuclear weapons program. Any future conflict on the peninsula seemed likely to involve North Korean use of chemical or nuclear weapons. North Korea tested a ballistic missile capable of reaching most of Asia and the Hawaiian Islands. In October 2006, North Korea declared that it had successfully conducted a nuclear test.

Nevertheless, the secretary of defense considered the situation stable enough to deploy Korea-based forces to Operation IRAQI FREEDOM. In 2004, the 2d Infantry Division deployed its 2d Brigade Combat Team to Iraq, the first out-of-area deployment of U.S. soldiers based in Korea. The brigade later redeployed to the United States, leaving the 2d Infantry Division with only one remaining brigade combat team. Nevertheless, the U.S. Army in Korea remained a lethal force. Between 2001 and 2003, the Eighth Army received the AH–64D Apache Longbow attack helicopter. Soldiers knew that war could erupt at any moment and that they would be involved from the opening minutes. They had to

85

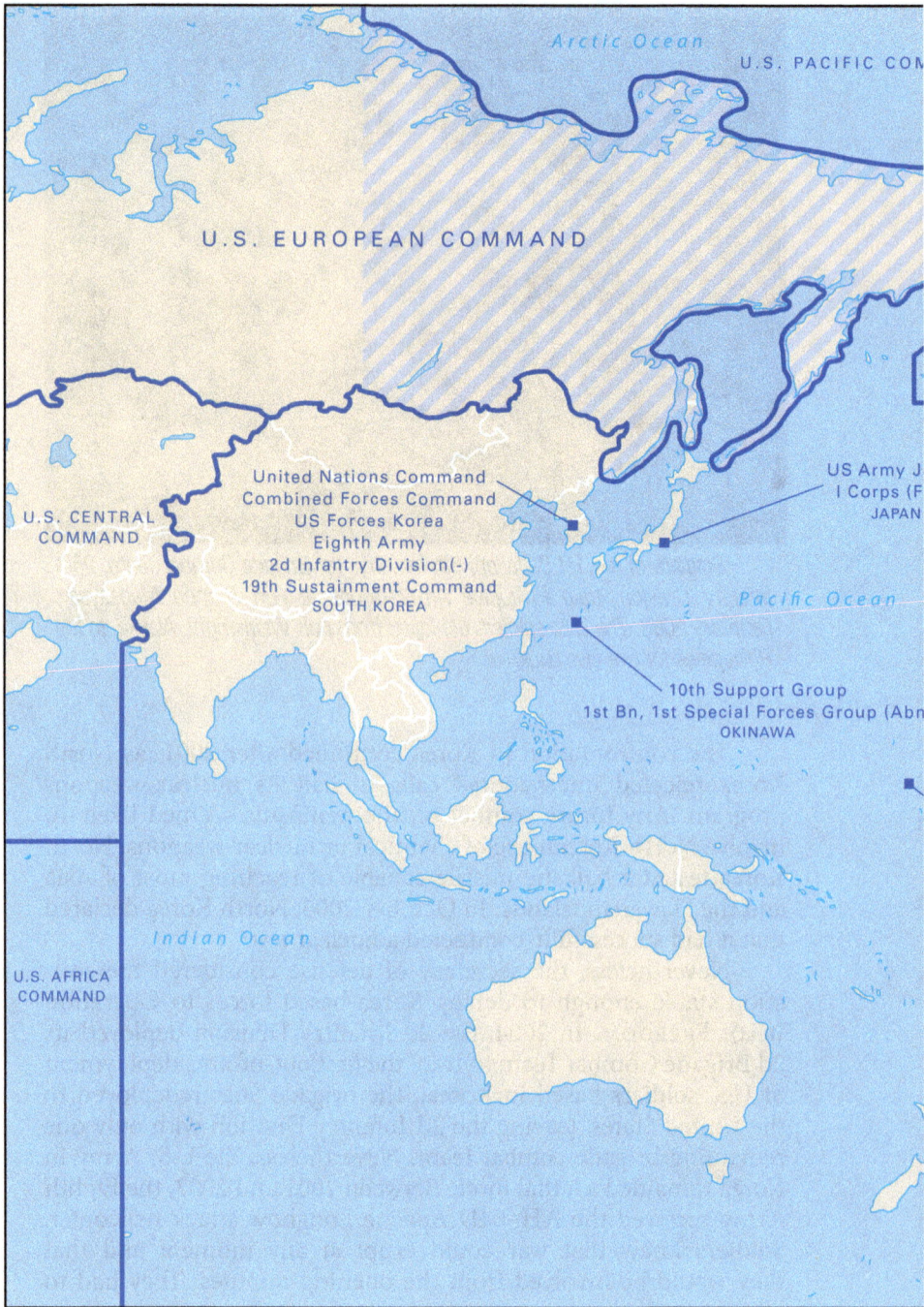

Arctic Ocean

U.S. PACIFIC CO[M]

U.S. EUROPEAN COMMAND

U.S. CENTRAL
COMMAND

United Nations Command
Combined Forces Command
US Forces Korea
Eighth Army
2d Infantry Division(-)
19th Sustainment Command
SOUTH KOREA

US Army J[
I Corps (F[
JAPAN

Pacific Ocean

10th Support Group
1st Bn, 1st Special Forces Group (Abn[
OKINAWA

Indian Ocean

U.S. AFRICA
COMMAND

Map 5

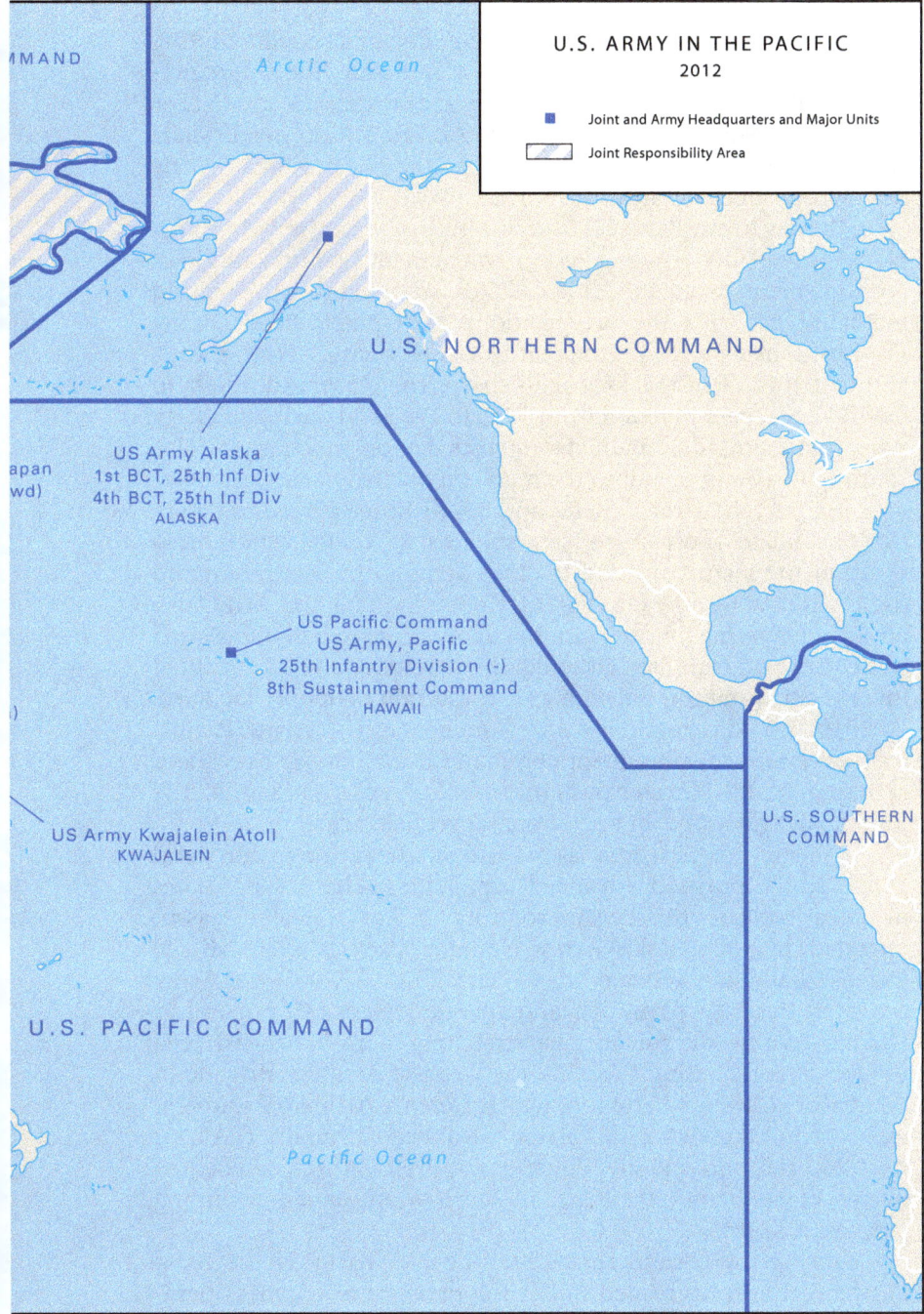

Arctic Ocean

MMAND

U.S. NORTHERN COMMAND

US Army Alaska
1st BCT, 25th Inf Div
4th BCT, 25th Inf Div
ALASKA

apan
wd)

US Pacific Command
US Army, Pacific
25th Infantry Division (-)
8th Sustainment Command
HAWAII

)

US Army Kwajalein Atoll
KWAJALEIN

U.S. SOUTHERN
COMMAND

U.S. PACIFIC COMMAND

Pacific Ocean

be prepared to "fight tonight" to defeat any attackers attempting to drive down the Uijeongbu corridor to Seoul. The unpredictable North Korean regime continued to threaten the south. For example, in November 2010 the U.S. Army's 210th Fires Brigade supported the South Korean force when the North Korean Army bombarded an island near the border.

The key to any battlefield success in Korea has always been the plans for reception, staging, onward movement, and integration of reinforcements from the United States. Arriving units rehearsed marrying up with the pre-positioned equipment from Army Pre-positioned Stock-4. Frequent exercises such as Foal Eagle and Ulchi Focus Lens kept skills sharp. The U.S. commitment to South Korea, paid in blood from 1950 to 1953 and during the sixty years that followed, remained strong, as demonstrated by the U.S. "putting its young men into the mud" on that troubled peninsula.

In 2002, the United States and South Korea agreed to a plan to consolidate most American soldiers at Camp Humphreys south of the Han River and to close Yongsan in Seoul, home to the Eighth Army and U.S. Forces, Korea. In 2008, the Army also began considering longer tours and allowing up to half of assigned soldiers to bring families, although this would require a substantial investment in family housing and community support facilities. By 2010, this construction was well under way. U.S. Army, Pacific, took over service component command functions for Korea and activated the 8th Theater Sustainment Command in Hawaii. The Eighth Army became an operational-level field army.

Ballistic missiles grew as a regional concern as China and North Korea pursued advanced capabilities. The United States installed ballistic missile interceptors at Fort Greely, Alaska, operated by the Alaska Army National Guard's 49th Missile Defense Battalion, activated in January 2004. In 2005, the Army activated the 94th Army Air and Missile Defense Command in Hawaii, responsible for an area stretching from Northeast Asia to Okinawa, including the 35th Air Defense Artillery Brigade in South Korea. The 1st Battalion, 1st Air Defense Artillery Regiment, was sent to Okinawa with Patriot Advanced Capability (PAC–3) missiles. Ballistic missile defense required an unprecedented degree of cooperation among all services and allies, including Japan and Korea.

During the decade after 2001, the U.S. Army in the Asia-Pacific region transformed under the pressure of combat operations and active security cooperation missions. Units reorganized into modular brigades and trained for network-centric operations. One brigade in Hawaii and one in Alaska converted to Stryker brigade combat teams. U.S. Army, Pacific, organized a contingency command post. Through it all, they provided deterrence and stability for a dynamic region that was inextricably linked to the United States and its future. *(Map 5)*

In the fall of 2011 during an address to the Australian Parliament, President Barack Obama announced a strategic "pivot" to the region and tacitly acknowledged the importance of the U.S. Army in the region for more than a century:

> Our new focus on this region reflects a fundamental truth—the United States has been, and always will be, a Pacific nation. Asian immigrants helped build America, and millions of American families, including my own, cherish our ties to this region. From the bombing of Darwin to the liberation of Pacific islands, from the rice paddies of Southeast Asia to a cold Korean Peninsula, generations of Americans have served here, and died here—so democracies could take root; so economic miracles could lift hundreds of millions to prosperity. Americans have bled with you for this progress, and we will not allow it—we will never allow it to be reversed.

During a century of engagement in the Asia-Pacific region, the U.S. Army became a global expeditionary force. It deterred conflicts, and when deterrence failed, it defeated America's enemies and supported its allies. It fought alongside allies and sister services in the Philippines, on Pacific islands, in Burma, Thailand, Korea, and Vietnam. It conducted occupations, led nation building, and eased human suffering. Under its protection, democracies took root and economies prospered, thanks to the selfless service and courage of generations of American soldiers. The U.S. Army played a vital and stabilizing role in the evolution of the Asia-Pacific region during a turbulent century.

FURTHER READINGS

Blair, Clay. *The Forgotten War: America in Korea, 1950–1953*. New York: Times Books, 1987.

Herring, George C. *America's Longest War: The United States and Vietnam, 1950–1975*. New York: Knopf, 2001.

James, D. Clayton. *The Years of MacArthur*. 3 vols. Boston: Houghton Mifflin, 1970–1985.

Linn, Brian McAllister. *The Philippine War, 1899–1902*. Lawrence: University Press of Kansas, 2000.

————. *Guardians of Empire: The U.S. Army and the Pacific, 1902–1940*. Chapel Hill: University of North Carolina Press, 1997.

McDonough, James R. *Platoon Leader*. Novato, Calif.: Presidio Press, 1985.

Moore, Harold G., and Joseph L. Galloway. *We Were Soldiers Once . . . and Young: Ia Drang, the Battle That Changed the War in Vietnam*. New York: Random House, 1992.

Spector, Ronald H. *Eagle Against the Sun: The American War with Japan*. New York: Free Press, 1985.

————. *In the Ruins of Empire: The Japanese Surrender and the Battle for Postwar Asia*. New York: Random House, 2007.

Stueck, William. *Rethinking the Korean War: A New Diplomatic and Strategic History*. Princeton: Princeton University Press, 2002.

Tuchman, Barbara W. *Stilwell and the American Experience in China, 1911–45*. New York: Macmillan, 1971.